NEW HAVEN FREE PUBLIC LIBRARY

3 5000 09554 4390

P9-AQG-065

New Haven Free
Public Library
133 Elm St.
New Haven, CT
06510

POETRY ROCKS!

ConTemporary American PoeTry

"Not the END, But the BegiNNing"

Sheila Griffin Llanas

Enslow Publishers, Inc.
40 Industrial Road
Box 398
Berkeley Heights, NJ 07922
USA
http://www.enslow.com

"A poem is not the end, but the beginning, of an excursion."
—William Stafford

Copyright © 2010 by Sheila Griffin Llanas

All rights reserved.

No part of this book may be reproduced by any means
without the written permission of the publisher.

Library of Congress Cataloging-in-Publication Data

Llanas, Sheila Griffin.
    Contemporary American poetry-"not the end, but the beginning" / Sheila Griffin Llanas.
        p. cm. — (Poetry rocks!)
    Includes bibliographical references and index.
    Summary: "Discover some of the poetry of leading contemporary American poets, including:
Roethke, Bishop, Stafford, Lowell, Brooks, Wilbur, Ginsberg, Merwin, Plath, Collins, and
Gluck"—Provided by publisher.
    ISBN-13: 978-0-7660-3279-8 (alk. paper)
    ISBN-10: 0-7660-3279-5 (alk. paper)
    1. American poetry—20th century—History and criticism—Juvenile literature.
2. American poetry—21st century—History and criticism—Juvenile literature. 3. Poets,
American—20th century—Biography—Juvenile literature. 4. Poets, American—21st century—
Biography—Juvenile literature. 5. American poetry—Explication—Juvenile literature.
6. Poetry—Authorship—Juvenile literature. I. Title.
    PS325.L63 2010
    811'.5409—dc22   2009023802

Paperback ISBN 978-1-59845-380-5

Printed in the United States of America
042011 Lake Book Manufacturing, Inc., Melrose Park, IL

10 9 8 7 6 5 4 3

To Our Readers: We have done our best to make sure all Internet addresses in this book were active and appropriate when we went to press. However, the author and the publisher have no control over and assume no liability for the material available on those Internet sites or on other Web sites they may link to. Any comments or suggestions can be sent by e-mail to comments@enslow.com or to the address on the back cover. Every effort has been made to locate all copyright holders of material used in this book. If any errors or omissions have occurred, corrections will be made in future editions.

♻ Enslow Publishers, Inc., is committed to printing our books on recycled paper. The paper in every book contains 10% to 30% post-consumer waste (PCW). The cover board on the outside of each book contains 100% PCW. Our goal is to do our part to help young people and the environment too!

Illustration Credits: Associated Press, pp. 32, 56, 70, 97, 120, 133; Clipart.com, p. 139; Everett Collection, pp. 20, 44, 63, 94, 108, 114; The Granger Collection, p. 9; iStockPhoto.com, pp. 1, 5, 8, 19, 31, 42, 55, 69, 82, 96, 106, 118, 132; Library of Congress, p. 84; Laura Jean Moore, p. 125; Photos.com, p. 26.

Cover Illustration: iStockphoto.com.

Contents

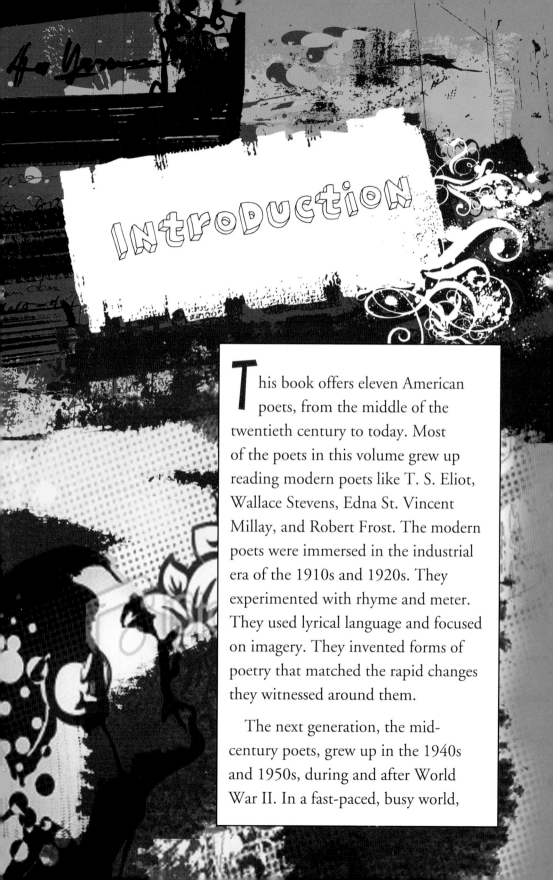

INTRODUCTION

This book offers eleven American poets, from the middle of the twentieth century to today. Most of the poets in this volume grew up reading modern poets like T. S. Eliot, Wallace Stevens, Edna St. Vincent Millay, and Robert Frost. The modern poets were immersed in the industrial era of the 1910s and 1920s. They experimented with rhyme and meter. They used lyrical language and focused on imagery. They invented forms of poetry that matched the rapid changes they witnessed around them.

The next generation, the mid-century poets, grew up in the 1940s and 1950s, during and after World War II. In a fast-paced, busy world, some people felt an increasing sense of alienation. Social movements exploded in the 1960s and 1970s. People fought hard for race and gender equality. Young people rejected social conformity that felt repressive. Once again, poets changed their form of expression to reflect the world around them. Poets expressed themselves freely. Rhyme and meter grew even more subverted.

The Beat poet Allen Ginsberg had a highly charged voice. His long poem "Howl" rocked the literary world. Robert Lowell and Sylvia Plath wrote confessional poems about their personal lives. W. S. Merwin wrote lyric poetry, formed by sound and image. Gwendolyn Brooks opened doors for young African American poets.

FACTS

A pattern of rhyming words is called a *rhyme scheme*. Rhyme schemes are identified by assigning a letter of the alphabet to each sound at the end of a line. For example, in Richard Wilbur's poem #23 from his book *Opposites*, lines one and two ("called" and "bald") rhyme, so both of those lines are assigned the letter *a*. The next two lines end with "hairy" and "necessary." They are assigned the letter *b* because they are different from *a* but similar to each other:

> Not to have any *hair* is called (*a*)
> *Hairlessness*, or being *bald*. (*a*)
> It is a fine thing to be hairy, (*b*)
> Yet it's not always necessary. (*b*)

Thus, the complete rhyme scheme is *aabb*.[1]

The number of American poets writing today is astonishing. Anthologies, literary magazines, and Web sites are filled with their work. This book of twelve poets—very few, relative to the number of accomplished poets writing today—offers an introduction to contemporary American poetry. We hope you will read more of each poet's work, and that you will seek out other poets to read. At the end of each chapter is a list of similar or related poets. We hope this book will be just the beginning of reading poetry for you.

1

Theodore Roethke

(1908–1963)

Theodore Roethke's father operated a greenhouse on the family's property in Saginaw, Michigan. Roethke (pronounced RET-key) grew up learning about bulbs, fertilizers, and seeds. He understood seasons, weather, and every aspect of growing plants. The farm was both a wonderful and a challenging place for a boy to grow up. Roethke loved flowers and trees, nature, and light. He was a lonely, introspective person. He delivered flowers and helped work his father's business. Roethke was fourteen, in 1923, when his uncle committed suicide. A few months later, his father died. Those early losses made a

Theodore Roethke

deep impression on him. He tried to shoulder the responsibility as head of the family.

Roethke received his undergraduate degree with honors from the University of Michigan in 1929. He went on to graduate school at Harvard, where he studied literature and began writing poems. He did not finish his master's degree. The Depression was on. Roethke left Harvard in 1931 to teach English for four years at Lafayette College in Easton, Pennsylvania, earning a hundred dollars a month. He published three poems in a little magazine called *The Harp*. At his next teaching job at Michigan State University, he drank too much, did not care for his health, and worked too hard. He was hospitalized for a mental breakdown. He lost his teaching job. After his release in January 1936, he continued to suffer breakdowns. Roethke probably suffered from bipolar disorder (then called manic depression), a condition that today could be managed with careful treatment.

He went on to teach at Pennsylvania State, in 1936, and published his first book, *Open House*, in 1941. In 1943, he taught briefly

FACTS

Roethke Reads

You can hear Theodore Roethke read "My Papa's Waltz" at the Web site of the Academy of American Poets.

at Bennington College.[1] Finally, he settled at the University of Washington, where he taught from 1947 to 1963. In 1953, he married Beatrice O'Connell, with poet friends Louise Bogan and W. H. Auden in his wedding party. He now had a reliable job and a supportive relationship. In 1954 his mother died. Just a few months later, he won a Pulitzer Prize for *The Waking*, published in 1953.

Roethke was a large man, over six feet tall. He was a passionate, theatrical teacher. He was popular with his students and had the reputation of being a "mad genius."[2] He lived intensely. He coached tennis, and he played tennis fiercely. He sometimes broke his rackets if he lost a tennis match. He formed important friendships with respected poets such as Rolfe Humphries, Stanley Kunitz, and William Carlos Williams. He met Humphries at a party near Easton. He showed up at Kunitz's door one day, wearing his fur coat, holding a stack of his poems.

One afternoon, at a party on Bainbridge Island, Washington, while swimming laps in an outdoor pool, Roethke suffered a heart attack and drowned. He was buried next to his parents in Oakwood Cemetery in Saginaw, Michigan. The day after his death, his friends had the swimming pool filled and created a memorial rock garden, a peaceful place to honor Roethke. Roethke's *Collected Poems* was published almost twenty years after his death, in 1982.

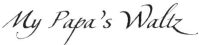

My Papa's Waltz

The whiskey on your breath
Could make a young boy dizzy;
But I hung on like death:
Such waltzing was not easy.

We romped until the pans
Slid from the kitchen shelf;
My mother's countenance
Could not unfrown itself.

The hand that held my wrist
Was battered on one knuckle;
At every step you missed
My right ear scraped a buckle.

You beat time on my head
With a palm caked hard by dirt,
Then waltzed me off to bed
Still clinging to your shirt.

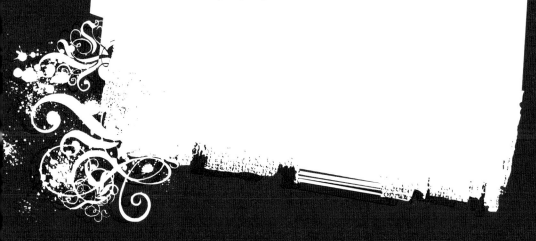

Summary and Explication: "My Papa's Waltz"

In "My Papa's Waltz," the speaker addresses his working-class father, recalling a time they danced in the kitchen together. It was a fairly wild dance. The father galloped around holding the boy. Perhaps the boy stood on his father's shoes as he "hung on like death." The boy's mother watched and frowned. Pans clattered to the floor.

The poem is in the past tense. The scene happened at night. It is the boy's bedtime. The father has been drinking, is possibly even drunk. The father's dance is playful, but it could also be hurting the boy.

Poetic Technique

The poem is like a dance. Though Roethke did not always use end-rhyme, this poem has an *abab* end-rhyme scheme. Roethke wanted this poem to sound like a child's nursery rhyme, since it is from a child's point of view. The title specifies the dance as a waltz. The lines have a buoyant, upbeat tempo. The rhyme and meter make this a fun poem fun to memorize and to recite. Even if the poem is negative, it is hard to read the poem in a sad voice. The tempo contrasts with the poem's dark themes.

Themes

"My Papa's Waltz" is one of Roethke's most well-known poems. It may or may not be an exact childhood memory. Roethke often explored his childhood to write his poems. He also often contrasted emotions. The first details of "My Papa's Waltz" convey both joy and fear: A waltz is joyous, but this dance may be hurtful or scary if the father is drunk. We do not really know whether the boy enjoys or endures his father's attention. Roethke did not explain whether the dance was playful or abusive. He did not judge or place blame. Instead, he made careful word choices and revealed small details about the boy and his father. These clues help the reader interpret the poem and come to his or her own conclusions.

Perhaps this poem succeeds because the answers to the questions it brings up are not obvious or simple. "My Papa's Waltz" is a good poem to discuss. Does the boy enjoy or resent this dance with his father? Is the experience frightening or exhilarating? Can it be both?

Roethke's Poetic Style

Roethke's childhood deeply influenced his writing. He believed that "to go forward as a spiritual man" and to grow, he had to look back.[3] Roethke had been a sad boy who grew up in lush nature. He was an emotional, intelligent, and creative person. His poems express the contrast he felt in his own life between emotions of joy and despair.

Having grown up on a greenhouse farm, it is no wonder that the language of plants infused his poetry. Nature fascinated him. Descriptions of nature appear in many poems. His book *The Lost Son* includes his "greenhouse poems" in which plants and roots become psychological metaphors. In long poems, with titles like "Journey to the Interior" and "The Longing," his natural images express his emotional experiences.

Roethke loved the musical sounds words made when put together. He liked internal rhyme, made with assonance and consonance. Roethke studied the rhyme and meter of poets from earlier eras like W. B. Yeats, John Donne, William Blake, and Walt Whitman. He imitated their work in order to craft his own style.

Old Florist

That hump of a man bunching chrysanthemums
Or pinching-back asters, or planting azaleas,
Tamping and stamping dirt into pots, —
How he could flick and pick
Rotten leaves or yellowy petals,
Or scoop out a weed close to flourishing roots,
Or make the dust buzz with a light spray,
Or drown a bug in one spit of tobacco juice,
Or fan life into wilted sweet-peas with his hat,
Or stand all night watering roses, his feet blue in rubber boots.

Discussion

If this poem were a photograph, you might see a stark contrast
between delicate flowers and the rough florist. The old man is not
idealized. What clues tell you about his character? Why did Roethke
end the poem with the man's blue feet in rubber boots? How do you
interpret that final image?

Roethke's poems are rich and musical. Notice the internal rhyme
in every line. In line 1, the words *hump*, *bunch*, and *mums* share the
same vowel sound. In line 2, the vowel sounds echo in *back*, *asters*,
and *planting*. What other internal rhyme do you find?

The Waking

I wake to sleep, and take my waking slow.
I feel my fate in what I cannot fear.
I learn by going where I have to go.

We think by feeling. What is there to know?
I hear my being dance from ear to ear.
I wake to sleep, and take my waking slow.

Of those so close beside me, which are you?
God bless the Ground! I shall walk softly there,
And learn by going where I have to go.

Light takes the Tree; but who can tell us how?
The lowly worm climbs up a winding stair;
I wake to sleep, and take my waking slow.

Great Nature has another thing to do
To you and me, so take the lively air,
And, lovely, learn by going where to go.

This shaking keeps me steady. I should know.
What falls away is always. And is near.
I wake to sleep, and take my waking slow.
I learn by going where I have to go.

Discussion

"The Waking" is a villanelle, a poetic form that is difficult and challenging to write. A villanelle has only two end-rhyme sounds. Lines 1 and 3 of the first stanza are repeated as refrains throughout the poem.

What do you think the repeated lines—"I wake to sleep, and take my waking slow" and "I learn by going where I have to go"—mean?

The speaker has a close relationship to nature. What does he learn from nature?

Epidermal Macabre

Indelicate is he who loathes
The aspect of his fleshy clothes, —
The flying fabric stitched on bone,
The vesture of the skeleton,
The garment neither fur nor hair,
The cloak of evil and despair,
The veil long violated by
Caresses of the hand and eye.
Yet such is my unseemliness:
I hate my epidermal dress,
The savage blood's obscenity,
The rags of my anatomy,
And willingly would I dispense
With false accouterments of sense,
To sleep immodestly, a most
Incarnadine and carnal ghost.

accouterments—items

incarnadine—blood-red or flesh-colored

carnal—relating to the body

Discussion

"Epidermal" means relating to skin; "macabre" means ghastly. "Epidermal Macabre" is both humorous and creepy. How could anyone dislike their own skin?

Read the poem aloud. How would you describe the voice? What makes the poem humorous?

Major Works by Theodore Roethke

Open House (1941)

The Lost Son and Other Poems (1948)

Praise to the End! (1951)

The Waking (1953)

Words for the Wind (1958)

I Am! Says the Lamb (1961)

The Far Field (1964)

Related Poets

As a teacher, Theodore Roethke was a role model and mentor. Roethke's students who went on to become published poets include Richard Hugo, James Wright, Carolyn Kizer, David Wagoner, Sandra McPherson, and Tess Gallagher.

2

ELIZABETH BISHOP
(1911–1979)

Born in Worcester, Massachusetts, Elizabeth Bishop was just a baby when her father died. Her mother never recovered. She wore black for five years and then entered a psychiatric hospital in 1916. Bishop never saw her again. Bishop lived a happy, quiet life with her mother's parents in Nova Scotia. She studied in a one-room schoolhouse. Her father's parents decided Bishop would be better off with them and, in 1917, took her back to Worcester. Bishop was unhappy there and grew sickly with asthma, eczema, and bronchitis. Life got a little better a year later when she went to live with an aunt in Boston. However, losing both

Elizabeth Bishop

her parents and having to move so often made Bishop feel lonely, displaced, and homeless.

At high school—a boarding school in Natick, Massachusetts, called Walnut Hill— friends called her "the Bishop." She had curly hair. She sang sea chanteys, ballads, and hymns. She published a few poems and made good friends. Though she was painfully shy, friends thought of her as funny, smart, and a good storyteller.[1]

Bishop studied at Vassar College, starting in 1930. While she was a student there, she admired the modernist poet Marianne Moore (1887–1972). A Vassar librarian lent Bishop her private copy of Moore's book *Observations* and arranged for Bishop to meet Moore. The two met outside the New York Public Library on March 16, 1934. They became friends and formed a lifelong literary bond. Moore became Bishop's mentor and encouraged her to write poetry. Bishop remained devoted to Moore for the rest of her life.

After Bishop graduated from Vassar in 1934, she traveled for ten years, using money from her father's estate. She loved the ocean and always lived near it. She eventually bought a house in Key West, Florida, but she still felt homeless. She continued to suffer problems such as asthma, depression, and alcoholism. In 1947, she met Robert Lowell at a party. He had written a review of her first book, *North & South*. They began to correspond. Lowell became another important and lifelong literary friend to Bishop.

In 1951, at age forty, she went to Brazil, intending only to visit. She had to stay when an allergic reaction to cashew fruit made her sick. A woman named Lota de Macedo Soares cared for Bishop. The two became close. Soares invited Bishop to live with her in a modern home in the mountains. She promised Bishop a writing studio. The home had lush views of gardens, mountains, and a waterfall. Bishop had finally found a home. She lived happily in Brazil for fifteen years. She wrote many poems during that time. When Soares died, Bishop was devastated. She wanted to live in the United States again, but where?

Her friend Robert Lowell invited Bishop to teach his classes at Harvard University for him while he went on leave. She taught poetry at Harvard from 1970 until 1977. She died suddenly of a cerebral brain hemorrhage in her Boston apartment. She had been scheduled to give a reading the following night. Instead, 750 people gathered and read Bishop's poems in her memory. She is buried in Worcester, Massachusetts.

FACTS

Listen to Bishop

You can find more poems by Elizabeth Bishop, and hear her read "The Armadillo," online at the Academy of American Poets.

Sandpiper

The roaring alongside he takes for granted,
and that every so often the world is bound to shake.
He runs, he runs to the south, finical, awkward,
in a state of controlled panic, a student of Blake.
The beach hisses like fat. On his left, a sheet
of interrupting water comes and goes
and glazes over his dark and brittle feet.
He runs, he runs straight through it, watching his toes.

—Watching, rather, the spaces of sand between them
where (no detail too small) the Atlantic drains
rapidly backwards and downwards. As he runs,
he stares at the dragging grains.

The world is a mist. And then the world is
minute and vast and clear. The tide
is higher or lower. He couldn't tell you which.
His beak is focussed; he is preoccupied,

looking for something, something, something.
Poor bird, he is obsessed!
The millions of grains are black, white, tan, and gray
mixed with quartz grains, rose and amethyst.

finical—finicky or particular

Blake–William Blake (1757–1827), English poet, painter, and
printmaker

Summary and Explication: "Sandpiper"

Bishop describes a small bird running on a beach, looking constantly at the sand at his feet. Bishop loved the ocean. She must have spent hours watching birds like this one. In her poem, the bird is only aware of the small view of the beach at his feet. The bird knows a lot about the grains of sand but very little about the ocean itself.

Poetic Technique

The poem has five four-line stanzas, also called quatrains. The rhyme scheme is *abcb* (in stanza two, it is *abab*), meaning that the end words in the second and fourth lines rhyme. While the first and third line end words do not rhyme exactly, they sound similar enough to be slant rhymes. Like most of Bishop's poems, "Sandpiper" is controlled and contained. The writer observes the bird from an objective, almost scientific, point of view.

However, that scientific viewpoint allows Bishop's gentle, dry humor to come through. She uses a serious tone to describe a crazy little bird. She teases a little when she compares the bird to "a student of Blake." Perhaps she meant that graduate students sift through tiny pieces of information, like sand. Sandpipers are fun to watch. Bishop captures what is most profound and comical about a sandpiper running crazily along the shore.

Themes

Many of Bishop's poems take place near water, on coasts, beaches, and along rivers. In the first line of "Sandpiper," Bishop gives the bird the ability to take the ocean for granted. Her description of the bird's behavior builds to an insight about the world in stanza four.

To say that the world is first a mist, then vast and clear, is an insight a human can have. Bishop gives the bird human qualities.

The bird looks endlessly for "something, something, something." The urgency of the line suggests a human impulse toward blind desire and restlessness. It was an emotion Bishop identified with. In a draft of a speech, Bishop once wrote, "All my life I have lived and behaved very much like that sandpiper—just running along the edges of different countries and continents, 'looking for something.'"[2]

Bishop's Poetic Style

Elizabeth Bishop, like her mentor Marianne Moore, loved to observe and describe nature. Nature awed her. Like Moore, she loved the sound words made together. Her style is unique and precise. She liked to describe exactly what she saw. She preferred literal to symbolic interpretations of poetry. She wanted her lines to mean what they said.

Bishop did not often write personal poems about her private life. She did not write confessional poems about her problems the way Lowell did. She sometimes wrote about events that happened to her. For example, in 1948, she published her poem, "Invitation to Miss Marianne Moore," in honor of her mentor. After Bishop had the chance to see the poet Ezra Pound in the mental hospital, she wrote the poem "Visit to St. Elizabeths."

Two of her descriptive poems, "In the Waiting Room" and "The Fish," tell a narrative story. The poems are based on events that happened in her life. In the first, she recalls being a girl of seven waiting in a dentist's office while her aunt had her teeth cleaned. The second tells of catching a large, old fish and observing it closely.

Many of her long poems, like "In the Waiting Room," build to an epiphany, an insight about herself and about life. For example, in her poem "The Fish," the speaker catches a huge fish and stares at it closely, face to face. When she sees five old hooks in its mouth, she realizes how much the old fish has survived. She feels a sense of triumph and lets the fish go. In a review of her first book, Lowell wrote, "Her descriptions … give body to her reflections, and her reflections … heighten her descriptions …" He called Bishop "one of the best craftsmen alive."[3]

Bishop's constant themes were her search for a home, her feelings of homelessness, and her love of travel. Some of her books have geographical titles—*North & South, Questions of Travel,* and *Geography III.* Lowell stated that Bishop "seldom writes a poem that doesn't have that exploratory quality; yet it's very firm, it's not like beat poetry, it's all controlled."[4]

During her life, although Bishop won many awards, she did not have a wide readership. She wrote slowly. Often several years passed between books. Her body of work is relatively small compared to that of some other writers. Since her death, her poetry has gotten more recognition.

Bishop used the description of the sandpiper to make a larger point about human behavior.

The Shampoo

The still explosions on the rocks,
the lichens, grow
by spreading, gray, concentric shocks.
They have arranged
to meet the rings around the moon, although
within our memories they have not changed.

And since the heavens will attend
as long on us,
you've been, dear friend,
precipitate and pragmatical;
and look what happens. For Time is
nothing if not amenable.

The shooting stars in your black hair
in bright formation
are flocking where,
so straight, so soon?
—Come, let me wash it in this big tin basin,
battered and shiny like the moon.

precipitate—hurried, thrown down, or fallen to earth

pragmatical—practical

amenable—agreeable, likable

ＤｉＳｃｕＳＳｉｏｎ

"The Shampoo" is one of Bishop's rare love poems. Through images, she makes enormous connections. She links lichen with the moon. She combines abstract Time with her friendship. She connects the night sky with the act of washing a friend's hair. Bishop enjoyed using scientific vocabulary. Even in this romantic poem, you can hear Bishop's crisp language in phrases like "precipitate and pragmatical."

How do the meanings of the word "precipitate" fit with Bishop's interconnected themes? What other words or phrases in her poem apply to both nature and relationships? How do the images of nature help the speaker express her feelings for her friend?

One Art

The art of losing isn't hard to master;
so many things seem filled with the intent
to be lost that their loss is no disaster.

Lose something every day. Accept the fluster
of lost door keys, the hour badly spent.
The art of losing isn't hard to master.

Then practice losing farther, losing faster:
places, and names, and where it was you meant
to travel. None of these will bring disaster.

I lost my mother's watch. And look! my last, or
next-to-last, of three loved houses went.
The art of losing isn't hard to master.

I lost two cities, lovely ones. And, vaster,
some realms I owned, two rivers, a continent.
I miss them, but it wasn't a disaster.

—Even losing you (the joking voice, a gesture
I love) I shan't have lied. It's evident
the art of losing's not too hard to master
though it may look like (Write it!) like disaster.

DiscuSSion

Bishop suffered early loss in childhood. "One Art" is a villanelle, and it has Bishop's characteristic gentle humor. She refers to loss as an art that a person could learn. Her writing is objective. She has no self-pity. The speaker seems to try to convince herself that loss is not a disaster—but is the speaker convinced? Notice the progression of items lost. They build from door keys, to cities, to "you." What purpose does the progression serve?

Major Works by ElizabeTh Bishop

Poetry

North & South (1946)
Poems (1956)
Questions of Travel (1965)
The Complete Poems (1969)
Poem (1973)
Geography III (1977)
The Complete Poems 1927–1979 (1983)

Prose

Brazil (1962
The Collected Prose (1984))

ReLaTed PoeTs

Bishop's work was praised by her peers and friends Robert Lowell and Randall Jarrell. Her work influenced poets such as John Ashbery (1927–) and James Merrill (1926–1995).

3

WILLIAM STAFFORD

(1914–1993)

William Stafford was born in Hutchinson, Kansas, the oldest of three children. During the Depression, his family traveled from one small Kansas town to another so his father could find work. Stafford earned money to help out. He delivered newspapers, picked sugar beets, and assisted an electrician. In rural Kansas, he camped, fished, and hunted. He loved the serenity and expansiveness of the earth. Stafford learned to value books from his parents, who both loved to read.

He graduated from high school in Liberal, Kansas, in 1933. He went on to the University of Kansas, earning his B.A. in 1937. He wanted to

William Stafford

become a writer. First, though, he was drafted into service when America entered World War II. He did not fight, however. Stafford was a pacifist. He believed in nonviolence. He was classified as 4E, a conscientious objector (CO). Rather than become a soldier, he worked in a Civilian Public Service (CPS) camp. He put out fires, built roads, planted trees, and terraced land in Arkansas, Illinois, and California. After long days of such hard work, he was too tired to write at night. Every morning, he woke before the sun came up and wrote. He kept this habit for the rest of his life.

Being a conscientious objector could be lonely. He lost friends who disagreed with his beliefs. COs were called "conchies" and accused of being spies or communists. One benefit was that Stafford met his wife, Dorothy, when she visited his CPS camp with her minister father. They married in 1944 and raised four children in their home in Lake Oswego, Oregon, a place that figured in his poetry. Stafford taught English at Lewis and Clark College in Portland, Oregon. In the 1950s, he earned a Ph.D. in creative writing from the University of Iowa.

He published his first book of poems when he was forty-six years old. He went on to publish more than sixty-five books of poetry and prose. In 1970, he became the United States poet laureate. In 1975, he was named poet laureate of Oregon. He retired from teaching in 1980. On the last day of his life, at age seventy-nine, he woke up early and wrote a poem. He died later of a sudden heart attack.

Fifteen

South of the bridge on Seventeenth
I found back of the willows one summer
day a motorcycle with engine running
as it lay on its side, ticking over
slowly in the high grass. I was fifteen.

I admired all that pulsing gleam, the
shiny flanks, the demure headlights
fringed where it lay; I led it gently
to the road and stood with that
companion, ready and friendly. I was fifteen.

We could find the end of a road, meet
the sky on out Seventeenth. I thought about
hills, and patting the handle got back a
confident opinion. On the bridge we indulged
a forward feeling, a tremble. I was fifteen.

Thinking, back farther in the grass I found
the owner, just coming to, where he had flipped
over the rail. He had blood on his hand, was pale–
I helped him walk to his machine. He ran his hand
over it, called me good man, roared away.

I stood there, fifteen.

Summary and Explication: "FifTeen"

The speaker of "Fifteen" tells the story of a day he found a fallen motorcycle, engine running. He paid a lot of attention to the bike. He was naïve enough to think he might be able to ride, perhaps even own, the bike. It took a long time for him to think of the bike's owner. Only by "thinking," in stanza four, did he realize that a fallen, still-running bike was obviously the scene of an accident. The boy seemed more disappointed than frightened by the accident. He wanted an adventure, not a chance to do a good deed.

PoeTic Technique

"Fifteen" is a narrative. It has a strong story, one that is very straightforward. The poem is in the past tense. We know the speaker is retelling what happened. He was fifteen at the time, but we do not know how old he is now. If you look deeper, you can find a metaphorical meaning. In a play on words, "Fifteen" takes place on a bridge on Seventeenth Street, as if the speaker stands between childhood and adulthood. The speaker imagined that, riding the bike, he "could meet the sky out on Seventeenth."

In this case, the speaker and the author are not one and the same. Stafford allows readers to consider the boy's character, to decide what kind of person he is and how this event changed him. The speaker's last line is, "I stood there, fifteen." Why did Stafford end the poem this way? How do you think this event affected the speaker?

Themes

Stafford often used the image of the sky in his poems, perhaps to represent freedom and eternity. "Fifteen" could be about a boy who wants a more expansive experience of life, a boy who wants the freedom he thinks adulthood will offer. "Fifteen" is not the only poem by Stafford in which a speaker comes upon the scene of an accident. "Traveling Through the Dark" is one of Stafford's most well-known poems. Find it online or in a book of his poems. In both poems, the speakers *think* and have to make a choice. Compare the speakers' decisions in "Fifteen" and "Traveling Through the Dark."

Stafford's Poetic Style

Stafford got up every day at 4:00 A.M. to write. During that quiet time in the morning, he trusted whatever ideas came to mind. He wrote notes to himself. He tried his ideas as poems. He never knew which ideas would become full-fledged poems. He was more interested in the writing process than in the finished product. In his essay, "A Statement on Life and Writings," he claimed he wrote "meandering sequences of thoughts, or spun-out patterns of words …"[1]

For Stafford, writing poems was like fishing. He waited for ideas to come. He wrote that most of his poems "came from free association, that is, free allowing of my impulses to find their immediate interest."[2] He claimed that he published only a fraction of what he wrote.[3]

In a time when some poets wrote pessimistic poems, Stafford wrote optimistic poems. Stafford used simple language and spare syntax. He did not force rhyme and meter into his lines. His poems may sound like they are easy to write. Stafford's son, in his memoir of his father called *Early Morning*, described the following scene at a poetry reading:

After my father had read a poem that seemed like simple talk, a voice blurted from the audience.

"I could have written that."

"But you didn't," my father said, looking down at the upturned face. He waited one beat of silence. "But you *could* write your own."[4]

Simple as they seem, Stafford's poems offer a deeper look at a complex world. He wrote about the mystery of nature. Many of his poems take place in the western United States. He wrote about family, childhood, and growing up. He also wrote about the mysterious process of self-awareness and humanity. He rarely made solid assertions about life. He suggested ideas. Stafford's poems function almost as parables, wrote Peter Stitt; they express symbolic, universal truths through story.[5]

FACTS

The Poet Laureate

Every year, a new United States poet laureate is appointed by the Librarian of Congress. (The official title is the Poet Laureate Consultant in Poetry to the Library of Congress.) During his or her term, the poet laureate represents and promotes poetry by giving readings, visiting schools, and establishing other ways for people to enjoy poetry, such as workshops, Web sites, and public discussions.

The Little Girl by the Fence at School

Grass that was moving found all shades of brown,
moved them along, flowed autumn away
galloping southward where summer had gone.

And that was the morning someone's heart stopped
and all became still. A girl said, "Forever?"
And the grass said: "Yes. Forever." While the sky—

The sky—the sky—the sky.

Discussion

This short poem (with a long title) tells an enormous story about life and death. The first stanza describes nature and seasonal change. The second stanza tells a "who, what, when" narrative with characters and dialogue

Stafford seems to imply that nature can answer difficult questions. The grass says something concrete. Why doesn't the sky? How do you interpret the last line?

School Play

You were a princess, lost; I
was a little bird. Nobody cared
where we went or how we sang.
A storm, I seem to remember, a giant
wave, some kind of crash at the end.
I think we cried when they took off our wings.

If time should happen again—and it could;
we're still in a play, you know—maybe
we'll hide so well the wave will pass
and after the storm we'll come out. We both
will really believe what, even then, we knew:
not the princess, not the bird—but the song—
was true.

Discussion

The first stanza of "School Play" is written as a childhood memory.
The second stanza is a reflection of the memory.

The speaker mentions a song at the end of the poem. What does
he mean by the word song? Why do you think he says that the *song*
was true?

Your Life

You will walk toward the mirror,
closer and closer, then flow
into the glass. You will disappear
some day like that, being
more real, more true, at the last.

You learn what you are, but slowly,
a child, a woman, a man,
a self often shattered, and pieces
put together again till the end:
you halt, the glass opens—

A surface, an image, a past.

Discussion

"Your Life" does not contain concrete imagery except for a
metaphorical glass mirror. It is an abstract poem about a process of
becoming self-aware. It has a slightly hypnotic feel, as if the reader is
being led to have a vision or an experience of his or her life.

What do you see in Stafford's mirror? What emotion does the
poem convey? Is it positive or negative?

Major Works by WilLiam STafford

Poetry

West of Your City (1960)

Traveling Through the Dark (1962)

The Rescued Year (1966)

Allegiances (1970)

Someday, Maybe (1973)

Stories That Could Be True (1977)

Things That Happen Where There Aren't Any People (1980)

Sometimes Like a Legend (1981)

A Glass Face in the Rain (1982)

Segues: A Correspondence in Poetry, written with Marvin Bell (1983)

The Way It Is: New and Selected Poems (1998)

Autobiography

Down in My Heart (1947)

ReLaTed PoeTS

If you like William Stafford, you might like Galway Kinnell (1927–), Gary Snyder (1930–), Raymond Carver (1938–1988), Marvin Bell (1937–), Ronald Wallace (1945–), and James Galvin (1951–).

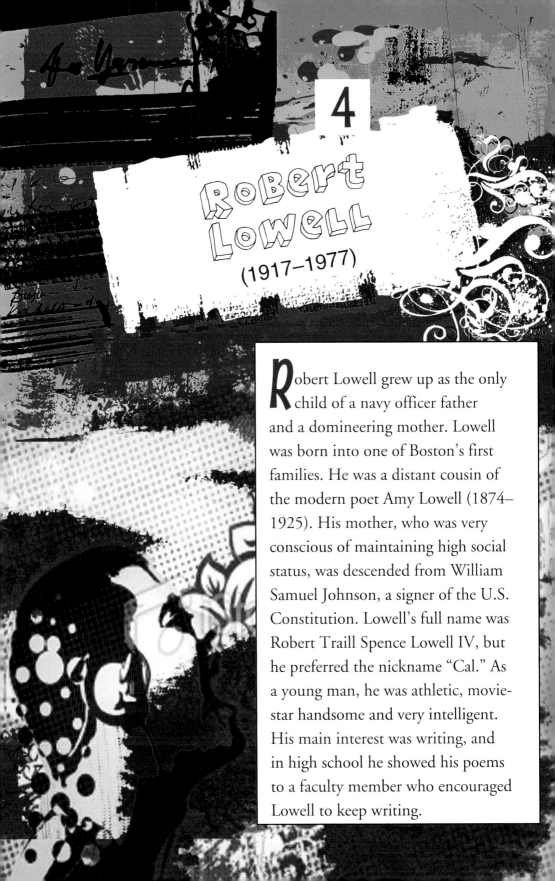

4

Robert Lowell
(1917–1977)

Robert Lowell grew up as the only child of a navy officer father and a domineering mother. Lowell was born into one of Boston's first families. He was a distant cousin of the modern poet Amy Lowell (1874–1925). His mother, who was very conscious of maintaining high social status, was descended from William Samuel Johnson, a signer of the U.S. Constitution. Lowell's full name was Robert Traill Spence Lowell IV, but he preferred the nickname "Cal." As a young man, he was athletic, movie-star handsome and very intelligent. His main interest was writing, and in high school he showed his poems to a faculty member who encouraged Lowell to keep writing.

Lowell started college at Harvard. His parents approved. Then he transferred to Kenyon College, in Ohio, because he wanted to study writing under the poet John Crowe Ransom (1888–1974). His parents were shocked. Lowell majored in the classics. He graduated summa cum laude, Phi Beta Kappa, and class valedictorian in 1940. Again, against his parents' wishes, Lowell took graduate courses at Louisiana State University. His parents did not like the school, but Lowell sought good poetry teachers.

Lowell wanted teachers so badly that he would show up on a poet's doorstep in order to meet him or her. Once, he barged in on Robert Frost, but the two poets did not connect. He traveled to Nashville, Tennessee, in 1937, to spend a day with Allen Tate. Lowell liked Tate so much that he returned for a longer stay. As the story goes, Tate's wife joked that the house was too crowded and if Lowell wanted to stay he would have to pitch a tent in the yard. She was joking. But Lowell went out, bought a pup tent, and camped on the Tates' lawn for a whole summer. Tate became one of Lowell's closest friends.[1]

Lowell's personal troubles, religious convictions, and political beliefs would all figure into his poems. His first marriage, to the novelist Jean Stafford, grew troubled, and they divorced. Lowell married the novelist Elizabeth Hardwick in 1949. They had one daughter, Harriet, in 1957. During World War II, Lowell protested America's bombing of German cities. When he refused to be drafted in 1943, he served time in jail. Years later, he spoke out against the Vietnam War.

He published his first major book of poems, *Lord Weary's Castle*, in 1946. The book earned Lowell a Pulitzer Prize. He had just turned thirty and had already become hugely successful.

Robert Lowell

Lowell struggled with bipolar disorder, then known as manic depression. He was hospitalized nine times for breakdowns. After *Lord Weary's Castle* appeared, he did not write for several years, until his psychiatrist suggested that as therapy he write about his childhood. Poems poured out of him. He crafted a new voice. He looked for help from William Carlos Williams, who believed poetry was a way to get feelings out. Lowell admired Williams's free writing style. It inspired him to develop his own unique style. Lowell visited Williams in Rutherford, New Jersey. The two poets became great friends. In 1959, Lowell published his book of autobiographical poems, *Life Studies*.

Lowell began teaching at Harvard. He was a popular, dynamic teacher. His students included Sylvia Plath and Anne Sexton. He won three Pulitzer Prizes and many other awards. At age sixty, Lowell died of a heart attack in a New York taxicab.

FACTS

Confessional Poetry

The critic M. L. Rosenthal called Lowell's book *Life Studies* "confessional." Rosenthal coined the phrase in his article "Poetry as Confession," first published in The Nation on September 19, 1959. Lowell's book *Life Studies*, as well as W. D. Snodgrass's book *Heart's Needle*, started the trend. Soon more poets began writing revealing autobiographical "I" poems as a way to process personal experiences with topics like death, depression, and relationships. The trend changed American poetry forever.

Skunk Hour

(For Elizabeth Bishop)

*Nautilus Island's hermit
heiress still lives through winter in her Spartan cottage;
her sheep still graze above the sea.
Her son's a bishop. Her farmer
is first selectman in our village,
she's in her dotage.*

*Thirsting for
the hierarchic privacy
of Queen Victoria's century,
she buys up all
the eyesores facing her shore,
and lets them fall.*

*The season's ill—
We've lost our summer millionaire,
who seemed to leap from an L. L. Bean
catalogue. His nine-knot yawl
was auctioned off to lobstermen.
A red fox stain covers Blue Hill.*

*And now our fairy
decorator brightens his shop for fall,
his fishnet's filled with orange cork,
orange, his cobbler's bench and awl,
there is no money in his work,
he'd rather marry.*

*One dark night,
my Tudor Ford climbed the hill's skull,
I watched for love-cars. Lights turned down,*

they lay together, hull to hull,
where the graveyard shelves on the town. . . .
My mind's not right.

A car radio bleats,
'Love, O careless Love . . . .' I hear
my ill-spirit sob in each blood cell,
as if my hand were at its throat . . . .
I myself am hell,
Nobody's here—

only skunks, that search
in the moonlight for a bite to eat.
They march on their soles up Main Street:
white stripes, moonstruck eyes' red fire
under the chalk-dry and spar spire
of the Trinitarian Church.

I stand on top
of our back steps and breathe the rich air—
a mother skunk with her column of kittens swills the garbage pail
She jabs her wedge-head in a cup
of sour cream, drops her ostrich tail,
and will not scare.

Queen Victoria's century—Queen Victoria was Britain's monarch
from 1837 to 1901.

Summary and Explication: "Skunk Hour"

"Skunk Hour" begins with a description of a decaying old Maine seaside town. The low point is buried in the middle of the poem. The speaker is miserable; he worries that his mind is not right. He feels completely alone. However, after a dramatic pause in the form of a stanza break, some skunks appear. They interrupt his melancholy monologue, and the poem. In a comical way, the skunks take his focus off of his psychological state.

Lowell makes the skunks sound like little monsters, invading the town during their one hour when they have the night to themselves. In the end, the mother skunk triumphs. Lowell "stands on top," at the beginning of the sixth stanza, but the mother skunk gets the last line. She will not "scare," meaning that Lowell may have tried to shoo her away. He was probably afraid of her, or at least respectful. Wouldn't you have been?

Poetic Technique

"Skunk Hour" is one of the first poems Lowell wrote in his search for a new style. He dedicated "Skunk Hour" to Elizabeth Bishop because when he read and reread her poems, he learned a new way to make line breaks. He liked her poem "The Armadillo" so much that he carried it around in his pocket with him. "Skunk Hour" is similar to "Armadillo," Lowell said, because both poems "use short line stanzas, start with drifting description, and end with a single animal."[2]

"Skunk Hour" has eight stanzas of six short lines each. The beginning meanders. Lowell said that he wrote the last four stanzas first, and then added the first four stanzas as a way to ease into the poem, to give it space. One way to read the poem is to imagine it like a scene in a movie. First the camera pans a coastal town from above. You see the water, the run-down houses, a few of the town characters who put on airs. The scene then zooms in on a single character and a specific scene. The first stanzas set the tone, but the poem gets direct and specific in stanza five starting with, "One dark night." That phrase lets you know a story is coming. That is when the poem's "I" speaker reveals himself and describes his lonely experience.

Themes

Lowell often wrote about decay. He felt that his parents' world of tradition was decaying and crumbling. He wrote about psychological states of mind. When this poem was published, Lowell's confession that "my mind's not right" was a bit shocking. People did not talk about mental illness.

Lowell admits that he wanted humor in "Skunk Hour." Skunks are cute but have a powerful form of self-protection. The nocturnal animals come out at night to dig in garbage. Lowell might have been comparing himself, ironically, to a skunk. After all, there he is, all alone, outside, digging around in his personal garbage, in the middle of the night, the time when skunks usually have the town all to themselves, the skunk hour.

Lowell's Poetic Style

After writing early poems with regular rhyme and meter, Lowell searched for a new style. When he wrote as therapy, and reviewed his childhood, he made his spectacular leap in his book *Life Studies*. *Life Studies* caused a revolution. It changed American poetry. At the time, no poet had written such raw autobiographical poems. No one had written about childhood like that before. Many poets had written

"I" poems, but the "I" was often a created persona. When Robert Lowell said "I," he meant himself. Lowell's style of writing was called "confessional." Critics hailed *Life Studies* as the most important book of the era.

Not everyone liked Lowell's new confessional poems. Even his best friend Allen Tate urged him not to publish them. Other critics complained that Lowell mocked and belittled his parents and their tradition. One critic said *Life Studies* described the moral collapse of Lowell's family. In later books, Lowell wrote sonnets that overtly exposed his marital problems with Hardwick. M. L. Rosenthal, who called *Life Studies* "a beautifully articulated poetic sequence" also said it was "rather shameful" to reveal personal family history.[3]

Elizabeth Bishop thought the poems had more social importance. She said they were about more than just his private life. She wrote that Lowell's poems tell us a lot "about the state of society."[4] If *Life Studies* was the first book of confessional poetry, it also began the debate about the value of confessional poetry.

Lowell used dark images of decay. He often remembered objects from his childhood as vividly as events. His word choices made objects sound violent, psychological, and dark. In "My Last Afternoon with Uncle Devereux Winslow," for example, Lowell recalls being five when his uncle died of Hodgkin's lymphoma. In one image, Lowell describes a large cuckoo clock carved with animals as "slung with strangled, wooden game." In this way, Lowell stripped away his family's regal majesty. He viewed the world of money and tradition that his parents tried to maintain as false and stuffy.

He still loved poetic tradition. He would never write as freely as the Beat poets, but he realized that his rhyme and meter were too strict, too traditional. He called his old poems "prehistoric monsters dragged down into the bog and death by their ponderous armor. I was reciting what I no longer felt."[5] Lowell owed a lot to William Carlos Williams for helping him craft the new style he used in *Life Studies*.

Lowell, often called the best poet of his generation, was a prolific writer. His *Collected Poems* is close to a thousand pages long. Lowell practiced many poetic styles. He closely studied and imitated great poets. Each of his books has a different style. In content, however, Lowell always focused on the theme of history, both public and personal, and the overlap between them. He made history by writing about his personal life.

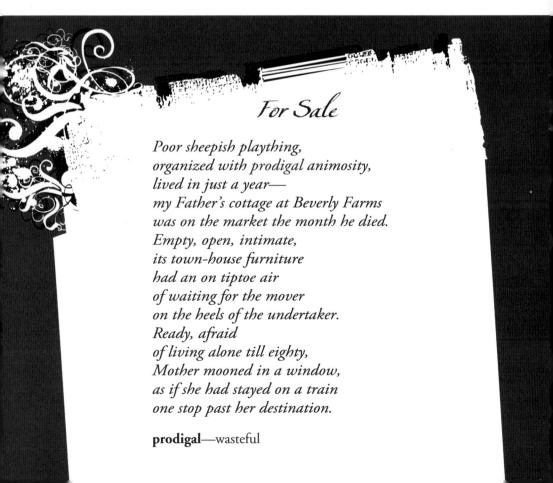

For Sale

Poor sheepish plaything,
organized with prodigal animosity,
lived in just a year—
my Father's cottage at Beverly Farms
was on the market the month he died.
Empty, open, intimate,
its town-house furniture
had an on tiptoe air
of waiting for the mover
on the heels of the undertaker.
Ready, afraid
of living alone till eighty,
Mother mooned in a window,
as if she had stayed on a train
one stop past her destination.

prodigal—wasteful

Discussion

Lowell describes a personal scene of sadness and loss in "For Sale." His father has died and a vacation cottage is being sold. Lowell ends the poem, however, with an image of his mother.

Does the image show Lowell's compassion for his mother, or does it make her look foolish? Do you think it was fair of Lowell to write this poem?

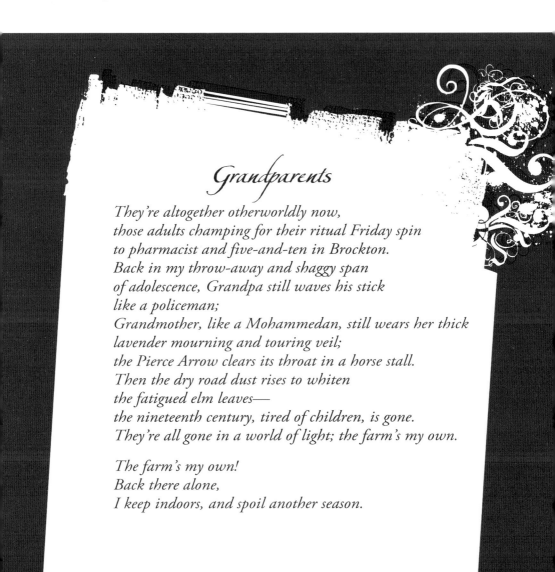

Grandparents

They're altogether otherworldly now,
those adults champing for their ritual Friday spin
to pharmacist and five-and-ten in Brockton.
Back in my throw-away and shaggy span
of adolescence, Grandpa still waves his stick
like a policeman;
Grandmother, like a Mohammedan, still wears her thick
lavender mourning and touring veil;
the Pierce Arrow clears its throat in a horse stall.
Then the dry road dust rises to whiten
the fatigued elm leaves—
the nineteenth century, tired of children, is gone.
They're all gone in a world of light; the farm's my own.

The farm's my own!
Back there alone,
I keep indoors, and spoil another season.

I hear the rattly little country gramophone
racking its five foot horn:
"Oh Summer Time!"
Even at noon here the formidable
Ancien Régime still keeps nature at a distance. Five
green shaded light bulbs spider the billiards-table;
no field is greener than its cloth,
where Grandpa, dipping sugar for us both,
once spilled his demitasse.
His favorite ball, the number three,
still hides the coffee stain.
Never again
to walk there, chalk our cues,
insist on shooting for us both.
Grandpa! Have me, hold me, cherish me!
Tears smut my fingers. There
half my life-lease later,
I hold an Illustrated London News—;
disloyal still,
I doodle handlebar
mustaches on the last Russian Czar.

Pierce Arrow—an antique car

Ancien Régime—literally, the political structure of France
before the revolution; a system no longer in force

Discussion

The first stanza of "Grandparents" describes the old world of
Lowell's ancestors. It ends with "the farm's my own." At the
beginning of the second stanza, Lowell delights, at first, in having the
farm to himself. But then he regresses back to being a child when life
was not perfect. He finds the stains and smudges of mistakes.

What elements of comedy does Lowell include in the poem? How
does Lowell make use of objects he remembers from his childhood?

Major Works by Robert Lowell

Lord Weary's Castle (1946)

The Mills of the Kavanaughs (1951)

Life Studies (1959)

Imitations (1961)

For the Union Dead (1964)

For Lizzy and Harriet (1973)

History (1973)

The Dolphin (1973)

Selected Poems (1976)

Day by Day (1977)

Related Poets

Another one of the first important books of confessional poetry was *Heart's Needle* by W. D. Snodgrass. Read the poetry of Lowell's good friends Allen Tate, Randall Jarrell, John Berryman, Elizabeth Bishop, and Delmore Schwartz. As a teacher, Lowell influenced his students, including Sylvia Plath and Anne Sexton.

Gwendolyn Brooks

(1917–2000)

Gwendolyn Brooks, born in Topeka, Kansas, grew up in Chicago, Illinois. She had one younger brother. Her father was the son of a runaway slave. Her parents struggled to achieve their dreams. Her father dreamed of becoming a doctor. Her mother wanted to be a concert pianist. Due to financial problems, her father became a janitor and her mother a teacher.

However, in her autobiography Brooks recalls a happy childhood. She grew up in a loving home, surrounded by aunts and uncles, filled with festive holiday celebrations. Her attentive parents taught her to memorize and recite poetry. Brooks published her

Gwendolyn Brooks

first poem, called "Eventide," in *American Childhood*, when she was only thirteen. Her proud mother said she would be "the *lady Paul Lawrence Dunbar*."[1] Dunbar (1872–1906) was one of the first African-American poets to gain recognition.

Brooks attended three different high schools, one mostly white, the next all black, and the last an integrated school. She was shy and withdrawn. It was hard for her to make friends at her schools. She chose to stay home and read rather than attend school dances. Writing made her courageous. She sent her poems to the poet James Weldon Johnson. She met Langston Hughes when he spoke in Chicago. Both poets encouraged her to keep writing. They were important writers of the Harlem Renaissance, a period in the 1920s and 1930s, when African-American artists living in Harlem created an outpouring of art and literature.

From age sixteen to eighteen, she published seventy-five poems in the black newspaper *The Chicago Defender*. She graduated from Woodrow Wilson Junior College (now called Kennedy-King College) in Chicago, in 1936. As a nineteen-year-old black woman in the middle of the Depression, Brooks knew it would be hard to find work.

She found community when she joined the Youth Council of the NAACP (National Association for the Advancement of Colored People, a civil rights group founded in 1909). There, she met Henry L. Blakely II, also a poet, when she was twenty-one. She married him two years later in 1939, in her parents' living room. In a time of shortage and racial discrimination, Brooks and her husband struggled to find good housing in poor areas of Chicago. They had two children, eleven years apart.

In spite of hardships, Brooks continued to write and to take poetry classes. Brooks began teaching poetry workshops in 1963. She started writing about her own life. She read the works of other black poets. She and her husband had a party for Langston Hughes, her childhood mentor, in their small apartment.

In 1967, Brooks attended a writers' conference at Fisk University. She met young black poets and learned new ideas about poetry and politics. After the conference, Brooks became involved in the Black Arts movement.

Brooks led workshops in her home for the young college students she met. Some students saw her views as old-fashioned and conservative. She saw their views as radical. They learned from each other. Two students, Haki Madhubuti (born 1942, formerly Don L. Lee) and Walter Bradford, became as close to her as her own

FACTS

The Black Arts Movement

The Black Arts Movement, or BAM, was started by the poet Amiri Baraka (formerly known as LeRoi Jones) after the assassination of Malcolm X in 1965. The movement encouraged African-American artists to write and form publishing houses rather than assimilate into the mainly white publishing industry.

children.[2] In 1990, Madhubuti founded the Gwendolyn Brooks Center for Black Literature and Creative Writing at Chicago State University.

In 1969, Brooks and her husband separated. Brooks enjoyed living alone, immersing herself in writing. She reunited with Blakely in 1973. They traveled to London, Ghana, and France. She turned down teaching jobs to write. She depended on the income she earned from her writing. She had a successful thirty-five-year career publishing with Harper & Row. Then she switched to Broadside Press in Detroit, one of the longest running African-American presses in the United States. Broadside published Brooks's *Riot,* which was about the assassination of Martin Luther King, Jr., the Chicago riots, and the civil rights movement.

Gwendolyn Brooks served as the Illinois poet laureate for thirty-two years, from 1968 until her death in 2000. She succeeded Carl Sandburg. From 1985 to 1986, she also served as U.S. Poet Laureate. She was invited to speak in schools and in prisons. She taught workshops. She established prizes and awards to help poets financially. She had a stroke and died at home surrounded by friends and family at age eighty-three.

Kitchenette Building

We are things of dry hours and the involuntary plan,
Grayed in, and gray. "Dream" makes a giddy sound,
not strong
Like "rent," "feeding a wife," "satisfying a man."

But could a dream send up through onion fumes
Its white and violet, fight with fried potatoes
And yesterday's garbage ripening in the hall,
Flutter, or sing an aria down these rooms

Even if we were willing to let it in,
Had time to warm it, keep it very clean,
Anticipate a message, let it begin?

We wonder. But not well! not for a minute!
Since Number Five is out of the bathroom now,
We think of lukewarm water, hope to get in it.

Summary and Explication: "Kitchenette Building"

"Kitchenette Building" takes place in a small apartment in a tenement building. The speaker must deal with paying rent, cooking food, and cleaning the home. What she really wants, however, is for her dream to be realized. She wonders if her dream can rise above her difficult conditions and circumstances. She switches back and forth between lofty ideals and mundane reality. Her "dream" competes with her conditions. The poem ends on a wry note of defeat. The concerns of daily life have won out. The speaker just wants to get some time in the shared bathroom. By the end, she does not even hope for a hot shower. The most she can hope for is lukewarm water.

Poetic Technique

The title declares the poem's setting and provides a visual image. Without knowing the title, the reader might not be able to make much sense of the first stanza. When you picture a woman sitting in her kitchenette apartment, however, you can visualize the scene. The speaker uses "we" rather than "I." She speaks for a community. She describes the reality of a group of people.

Brooks gives herself structural freedom. She adds an extra line to stanza two. For the other stanzas, she uses the unusual end-rhyme scheme *aba*. There are touches of humor, such as the rhyming of "minute" and "in it," and the image of a dream rising through onion fumes. Brooks's humor, however, comes with a touch of bitterness.

Themes

African-American families had trouble finding good housing in Chicago. Gwendolyn Brooks and her husband experienced this firsthand when they had to live in cramped apartments called kitchenettes. They lived in large complexes in a poor Chicago neighborhood. Their neighbors were families who also struggled to create safe, comfortable homes in poor conditions. Many poems in Brooks's book *A Street in Bronzeville* describe these people. They are descriptions of that reality, but they also make a social statement.

The idea of a "dream" may echo the themes of her mentor Langston Hughes, who also often wrote of having a dream. Like Hughes, Brooks does not define her dream in "Kitchenette Building." She does not limit the word by making it stand for any one specific thing. She wants, perhaps, to rise above daily impossibilities and injustices, and she also wants more than that. The expansive word "dream" makes her feel giddy, she says in line 2, but it is not as strong, for now, as the things that hold her down.

Brooks's Poetic Style

Brooks greatly admired the black poets of the Harlem Renaissance. However, it discouraged her that white audiences saw black people as "exotic." She wanted her poetry to humanize African Americans. "Miss Brooks is real and so are her poems," wrote Richard Wright, a reviewer of her first book, *A Street in Bronzeville*, which appeared in 1945.[3] The book describes Brooks's own Chicago neighborhood. She had seen tenement buildings replace residential homes. She gave "voice" to the residents of her neighborhood.

A Street in Bronzeville earned Brooks almost instant recognition. She got positive reviews and was named one of *Mademoiselle* magazine's "Ten Women of the Year." She won a Pulitzer Prize for her book *Annie Allen* at age thirty-three. She was the first African American ever to win a Pulitzer Prize.

After attending the Fisk University writers' conference in 1967, Brooks's priorities and writing style changed. She stopped writing formal poetry. She wanted her poetry to speak to black audiences. She wanted to reach people who had never been interested in poetry before.

Brooks with her first book of poems, *A Street in Bronzeville*.

We Real Cool

The Pool Players.
Seven at the Golden Shovel.

We real cool. We
Left school. We

Lurk late. We
Strike straight. We

Sing sin. We
Thin gin. We

Jazz June. We
Die soon.

Discussion

"We Real Cool" is one of Brooks's best-known poems. With eight lines and all single-syllable words, Brooks shows the power of a short poem. Her speaker is a collective "we." The pool players speak in chorus with no sense of individuality. The word "We" begins each sentence and ends every line except the last. Brooks said that the word "we" should be spoken softly, as if the pool players were uncertain of their identity.[4] Some readers hear bravado and defiance in the poem. Other readers hear defeat and destruction.

Listen to Brooks speak about and read "We Real Cool" at the Academy of American Poetry Web site. How does hearing Brooks read "We Real Cool" help you to interpret and appreciate the poem? How does the poem's shape and form add to its message?

The Crazy Woman

I shall not sing a May song.
A May song should be gay.
I'll wait until November
And sing a song of gray.

I'll wait until November.
That is the time for me.
I'll go out in the frosty dark
And sing most terribly.

And all the little people
Will stare at me and say,
"That is the Crazy Woman
Who would not sing in May."

Discussion

"The Crazy Woman" has a sing-song quality. It sounds like a nurse
rhyme. It has a note of defiance and rebellion, however. How woul
you describe the poem's strong-willed speaker? Based on what you
know about the speaker, why might she prefer November?

Big Bessie Throws Her Son
Into the Street

(excerpt from "A Catch of Shy Fish")

A day of sunny face and temper
The winter trees
Are musical.

Bright lameness from my beautiful disease,
You have your destiny to chip and eat.

Be precise.
With something better than candles in the eyes.
(Candles are not enough.)

At the root of the will, a wild inflammable stuff.

New pioneer of days and ways, be gone.
Hunt out your own or make your own alone.

Go down the street.

Discussion

The poem's title tells its story: A woman has kicked her son out of the house. The poem is a speech Big Bessie gives her son. She offers no other details about what happened. Her language sounds lyrical and metaphorical, like the language of the soul.

What does Big Bessie want for her son? How do you know? What does the speaker mean by the line, "Bright lameness from my beautiful disease"?

Major Works by Gwendolyn Brooks

Poetry

A Street in Bronzeville (1945)

Annie Allen (1949)

Bronzeville Boys and Girls (1956)

The Bean Eaters (1960)

We Real Cool (1966)

The Wall (1967)

In the Mecca (1968)

Family Pictures (1970)

Riot (1970)

Black Steel: Joe Frazier and Muhammad Ali (1971)

Aloneness (1971)

The World of Gwendolyn Brooks (1971)

Aurora (1972)

Beckonings (1975)

To Disembark (1981)

Black Love (1981)

The Near-Johannesburg Boy and Other Poems (1986)

Blacks (1987)

Winnie (1988)

Children Coming Home (1991)

Prose

Report from Part One: An Autobiography (1972)

A Capsule Course in Black Poetry Writing (1975)

Primer for Blacks (1981)

Young Poet's Primer (1981)

Very Young Poets (1983)

Report from Part Two: An Autobiography (1996)

Related Poets

The poet Elizabeth Alexander (1962–) edited *The Essential Gwendolyn Brooks* (Graywolf Press, 2005). She read at the presidential inauguration of Barack Obama in 2009.

You might also enjoy the poetry of Lucille Clifton (1936–), Audre Lorde (1934–1992), and Nikki Giovanni (1943–).

6

RICHARD WILBUR
(1921–)

When Richard Wilbur was born, his parents could see the Hudson River from their small New York City apartment. When he was two years old, the family, which now included a younger brother, moved from the city to a farm in New Jersey. Wilbur grew up learning to love nature and solitude.

In high school, Wilbur read the poets Robert Frost and Hart Crane. At Amherst College, Wilbur majored in English and liked stories he read about hobos. On summer breaks in the 1930s, he hopped freight trains and hitchhiked around the country. He called himself a "privileged hobo" because he had money to fall back on.[1]

Richard Wilbur

Wilbur began to study poetry seriously. He liked the close observation of the poetry of Marianne Moore, Elizabeth Bishop, and William Carlos Williams. He liked the way they could attach big ideas to small, simple objects. They said important things about common, ordinary life.

In college, Wilbur fell in love with a student named Charlotte Hayes Ward. She studied at Smith, an all-women's college, and Wilbur sometimes walked nine miles from Amherst to see her. After graduation, in June 1942, six months after the Japanese bombed Pearl Harbor, Wilbur and Charlotte married. Wilbur had to leave his new wife temporarily to serve in World War II as a cryptographer, a specialist in deciphering enemy codes. Transferred to the front lines, he fought in France, Italy, and Germany. Between periods of intense artillery fire, he read Edgar Allan Poe stories from a paperback book he kept in his pocket.

FACTS

Watching Wilbur

You can hear Richard Wilbur reading some of his poems and talking about translating poetry at the Web site of the Poetry Foundation.

Wilbur returned home to Charlotte in 1945. He studied at Harvard, earning a master's degree that would allow him to become a teacher. Two years later, at the age of twenty-six, he graduated from Harvard and published his first book, *The Beautiful Changes and Other Poems.* He had begun his career as a poet and a teacher.

Wilbur met Robert Frost. He impressed Frost because he knew so many of his poems by heart. Wilbur taught at Harvard until 1954, and then taught at Wellesley College and Wesleyan University. In 1957, he published *Things of This World,* a book that won a Pulitzer Prize, a National Book Award, and the Edna St. Vincent Millay Memorial Award. He helped found the Wesleyan University Press poetry series to publish new poets. He retired from teaching in 1986 and, in 1987, served for one year as the second U.S. poet laureate, after Robert Penn Warren. In 1988, he earned his second Pulitzer Prize for *New and Collected Poems.*

During a time in the 1960s and 1970s, when many poets succumbed to despair, depression, and destructive lifestyles, Wilbur worked on having a steady career and a healthy life. He loves playing tennis and enjoys gardening. He remains devoted to his wife, Charlotte. They raised four children. The couple still lives in their dream home in rural Massachusetts.

Love Calls Us to the Things of This World

The eyes open to a cry of pulleys,
And spirited from sleep, the astounded soul
Hangs for a moment bodiless and simple
As false dawn.
Outside the open window
The morning air is all awash with angels.

Some are in bed-sheets, some are in blouses,
Some are in smocks: but truly there they are.
Now they are rising together in calm swells
Of halcyon feeling, filling whatever they wear
With the deep joy of their impersonal breathing;

Now they are flying in place, conveying
The terrible speed of their omnipresence, moving
And staying like white water; and now of a sudden
They swoon down into so rapt a quiet
That nobody seems to be there.
The soul shrinks

From all that it is about to remember,
From the punctual rape of every blessèd day,
And cries,
"Oh, let there be nothing on earth but laundry,
Nothing but rosy hands in the rising steam
And clear dances done in the sight of heaven."

Yet, as the sun acknowledges
With a warm look the world's hunks and colors,
The soul descends once more in bitter love
To accept the waking body, saying now
In a changed voice as the man yawns and rises,
"Bring them down from their ruddy gallows;
Let there be clean linen for the backs of thieves;
Let lovers go fresh and sweet to be undone,
And the heaviest nuns walk in a pure floating
Of dark habits,
keeping their difficult balance."

halcyon—peaceful, joyful

omnipresence—present in every place at every time

Summary and Explication: "Love Calls Us To The Things of This World"

Imagine being woken from a deep sleep by a loud noise. "Love Calls Us to the Things of This World" begins abruptly. A person is torn from deep sleep by the squeak of pulleys. Outside the window are angels. At this point, the reader might be a little dazed. Wilbur wants his first stanza to convey the confusion of just waking up, a time when many people would rather remain "bodiless" and sound asleep.

In the second stanza, Wilbur explains that the angels are really pieces of clothing fluttering in the breeze, hanging on a laundry line outside a city tenement building (a common sight in the 1950s). The billowing bedsheets and empty blouses look like angels. A neighbor pulls the laundry in from a squeaky clothesline. In the end, the clean clothes, the "angels," come down from the line to be worn by ordinary people who express a variety of human behaviors and beliefs, ordinary people who try to keep "their difficult balance," perhaps between right and wrong, good and bad, body and soul.

Poetic Technique

The poem has no speaker. There is no "I." In that way, the poem is "bodiless." Wilbur refers to his subject as "one," as if what he describes could be anyone's experience. In a way, it does help the reader get inside the experience. There is no individual person to imagine.

This is one of Wilbur's few unrhymed poems. He gives the poem shape. His line breaks move spontaneously, almost like laundry fluttering in the air outside the window. Wilbur loved language play, puns, and double meanings. In stanza four, Wilbur uses the violent image "punctual rape" to describe the alarm clock. In his last sentence, nuns walk in "dark habits"—habits are the draped clothing worn by nuns but they are also repeated, conditioned human behaviors that are not always beneficial. It is hard to balance body and soul.

Themes

This exuberant, witty poem was written in 1956, the same year that Allen Ginsberg published *Howl*. Wilbur's poem connects the physical and the spiritual world. It captures a vision of daily reality the moment a person wakes up, a person who would rather stay asleep. Wilbur merged a lofty theme with the practical, earthly necessities. There is a longing to know the soul and to be free. However, people have to wake up every day and do work like folding laundry. The critic Donald Hill suggests that Wilbur's poems focus mainly on practical, worldly things because Wilbur wanted to, and was able to, accept the human condition.[2]

Wilbur's Poetic Style

Many poets change their style from book to book. Wilbur has not. He crafted a style and has continued to refine and master it throughout his long and steadily successful career. In a time when many poets take a pessimistic view of the world, America, and their own personal troubles, Wilbur writes uplifting poems about common, everyday experiences. Most of his poems are crafted with careful rhyme and meter. He likes wordplay and humor, puns and paradoxes. His books for children are based on wordplay.

Wilbur does not like abstract language. He likes clear, concrete subjects. He likes simple, ordinary events and objects. Wilbur admires Robert Frost, and he has studied the way Frost used a conversational tone in his rhyming poems.[3] Frost's poems can be easily understood on a first reading, Wilbur said, and added, "Then you read it a second time and you notice something more."[4] Wilbur strives for the same effect in his own writing. Theodore Roethke praised Wilbur, saying that he "can look at a thing, and talk about it beautifully, can turn it over in his mind, and draw truths from a scene, easily and effortlessly (it would seem)."[5]

About finding his own style, Wilbur said, in an interview in 1995, "The poetry that most appeals to me is the least abstract and the most inclusive. How I came to feel this way I can't really account for biographically. But I'm glad that it happened, because I approve of my taste."[6] Richard Wilbur is considered one of the top translators of poetry. He translated the work of poets such as Paul Valéry, François Villon, Charles Baudelaire, Anna Akhmatova, Joseph Brodsky, as well as French plays by seventeenth-century dramatists Molière and Jean Racine.

Mind

Mind in its purest play is like some bat
That beats about in caverns all alone,
Contriving by a kind of senseless wit
Not to conclude against a wall of stone.

It has no need to falter or explore;
Darkly it knows what obstacles are there,
And so may weave and flitter, dip and soar
In perfect courses through the blackest air.

And has this simile a like perfection?
The mind is like a bat. Precisely. Save
That in the very happiest intellection
A graceful error may correct the cave.

intellection—thought; reasoning

Discussion

Wilbur challenges himself to include a lot of elements in his poem.
In this one, he develops an extended simile of the mind as a bat,
and he uses the end-rhyme scheme *abab*. You will also notice a lot
of alliteration—both consonance and assonance. The words fit so
tightly together. Read the poem out loud to hear the sounds and
shapes the words make.

The Pardon

My dog lay dead five days without a grave
In the thick of summer, hid in a clump of pine
And a jungle of grass and honeysuckle-vine.
I who had loved him while he kept alive

Went only close enough to where he was
To sniff the heavy honeysuckle-smell
Twined with another odor heavier still
And hear the flies' intolerable buzz.

Well, I was ten and very much afraid.
In my kind world the dead were out of range
And I could not forgive the sad or strange
In beast or man. My father took the spade

And buried him. Last night I saw the grass
Slowly divide (it was the same scene
But now it glowed a fierce and mortal green)
And saw the dog emerging. I confess

I felt afraid again, but still he came
In the carnal sun, clothed in a hymn of flies,
And death was breeding in his lively eyes.
I started to cry and call his name,

Asking forgiveness of his tongueless head.
… I dreamt the past was never past redeeming:
But whether this was false or honest dreaming
I beg death's pardon now. And mourn the dead.

Discussion

In "The Pardon" Wilbur recalls a childhood memory and tells the story of losing his dog when he was too young to be able to deal with it appropriately. He writes his narrative poem in quatrains, with an end-rhyme scheme of *abba*.

What else is going on in the poem beyond its straightforward story?

In stanza four, the poem shifts in time. When the dog appears to the now-adult Wilbur in a dream, why do you think he asks his dog for forgiveness?

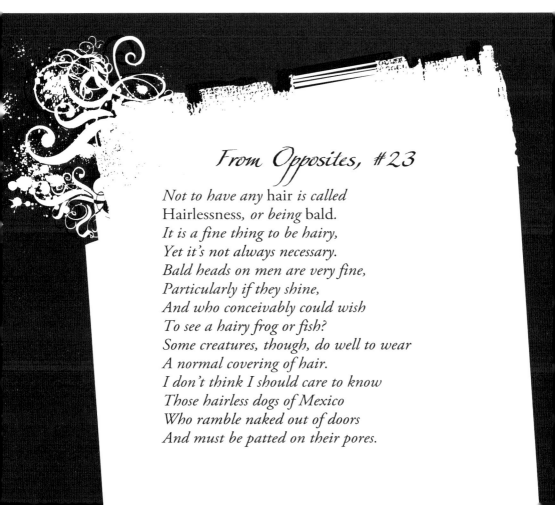

From Opposites, #23

Not to have any hair *is called*
Hairlessness, *or being* bald.
It is a fine thing to be hairy,
Yet it's not always necessary.
Bald heads on men are very fine,
Particularly if they shine,
And who conceivably could wish
To see a hairy frog or fish?
Some creatures, though, do well to wear
A normal covering of hair.
I don't think I should care to know
Those hairless dogs of Mexico
Who ramble naked out of doors
And must be patted on their pores.

Discussion

You can see Wilbur's way of thinking in the wordplay of #23 from his book *Opposites*. It is worth reading his series of humorous poems. You can find them at the end of *New and Collected Poems*. You might also find *A Pig in the Spigot* and *The Disappearing Alphabet* in the children's section of your public library.

How much of the humor in the poem is created with word associations rather than content information? Which lines provide the best example of word associations and why?

What is the value of humorous poems like this one?

Major Works by Richard Wilbur

The Beautiful Changes and Other Poems (1947)
Ceremony and Other Poems (1950)
Things of This World (1956)
Advice to a Prophet and Other Poems (1961)
Walking to Sleep: New Poems and Translations (1969)
The Mind-Reader: New Poems (1976)
New and Collected Poems (1988)
Opposites, More Opposites, and a Few Differences (2000)
The Pig in the Spigot (2000)
The Disappearing Alphabet (2001)

Related Poets

If you like Richard Wilbur, you might like some of the poets he helped publish in the Wesleyan University Press poetry series, such as Robert Bly, James Wright, James Dickey, and Richard Howard.

Allen Ginsberg

(1926–1997)

Allen Ginsberg was born to Jewish parents Louis and Naomi Ginsberg in Newark, New Jersey. The family soon moved to Paterson, New Jersey. Ginsberg's father taught and wrote poetry. His mother suffered from paranoid schizophrenia. Her behavior could be hard to manage. As a teenager, Ginsberg often stayed home from school to take care of her. In 1941, Naomi Ginsberg was hospitalized, treated with electroshock therapy, and given a lobotomy. Because of his mother's illness, Ginsberg had enormous compassion for people with mental disorders. As a young man, Ginsberg also struggled to

Allen Ginsberg

accept his homosexuality. These two things made him feel sensitive and insecure.

In high school, two of Ginsberg's favorite authors were Walt Whitman and Edgar Allan Poe. He met William Carlos Williams, an older poet who also lived in Paterson. In spite of his interest in poetry, in the 1940s Ginsberg went to Columbia University intending to become a labor lawyer. He wanted to help working-class people. His goals changed when he met major writers in what came to be called the Beat Generation—William Burroughs, Jack Kerouac, Gregory Corso, and Neal Cassady.

One night, Ginsberg had a dream about the poet William Blake (1757–1827; author of *Songs of Innocence* and *Songs of Experience* and other books). Ginsberg believed his vision, which he wrote about in his poem "Psalm IV," showed him his life's direction. He gave up studying law and committed himself to writing poetry.

In 1949, some of Ginsberg's friends hid stolen goods in his apartment. Ginsberg was arrested as an accessory to theft. He pleaded insanity and was sentenced to eight months in a psychiatric institute. There, he became close friends with a writer and fellow inmate named Carl Solomon. Ginsberg later dedicated "Howl" to Solomon and included some of the phrases Solomon said in the long poem.

On October 7, 1955, Ginsberg made literary history when he read his poem "Howl" at a poetry reading held at an art gallery called Six Gallery in San Francisco. He was twenty-nine. He had never read at a poetry reading before. He had written "Howl" only two weeks earlier. He started reading his long poem calmly but soon began to sway and sing the lines. Audience members were astonished by

Ginsberg's dramatic reading. They shouted, "Go! Go!" at the end of each long line. When he finished, people cheered. A few even cried. The reading was a turning point for American poetry. It launched both Ginsberg's career and the Beat Generation.

When his mother, Naomi, died in 1956, the grieving Ginsberg wrote a long poem called "Kaddish" in her memory. (Kaddish is the Jewish mourning prayer or blessing.) He revealed information about his family's history, especially about his mother's mental illness. Like Robert Lowell, Ginsberg was one of the first poets of the era to write and publish poems about private family problems.

Some poets crave solitude. Ginsberg, however, had an enormous community of friends. He mixed actively in social and popular culture. In 1954, Ginsberg met the poet Peter Orlovsky. The two fell in love and became lifelong partners. Ginsberg actively supported gay rights. He explored spirituality and studied Buddhism under Zen masters. In 1974, Ginsberg helped found the Jack Kerouac School of Disembodied Poetics at Naropa University, a Buddhist college in Boulder, Colorado. In the 1970s and 1980s Ginsberg recorded and toured with Bob Dylan, The Clash, and other musicians. Ginsberg enjoyed performing and reciting his poems. He played an accordion and wrote songs with titles like "Vomit Express" and "4 A.M. Blues." Although liver cancer made his last months uncomfortable, Ginsberg died peacefully in his New York loft apartment, surrounded by friends.

Excerpt from

Howl

I saw the best minds of my generation destroyed by
   madness, starving hysterical naked,
dragging themselves through the negro streets at dawn
   looking for an angry fix,
angelheaded hipsters burning for the ancient heavenly
   connection to the starry dynamo in the machinery
   of night,
who poverty and tatters and hollow-eyed and high sat
   up smoking in the supernatural darkness of
   cold-water flats floating across the tops of cities
   contemplating jazz,
who bared their brains to Heaven under the El and
   saw Mohammedan angels staggering on tenement
   roofs illuminated,
who passed through universities with radiant cool eyes
   hallucinating Arkansas and Blake-light tragedy
   among the scholars of war,
who were expelled from the academies for crazy &
   publishing obscene odes on the windows of the skull,
who cowered in unshaven rooms in underwear,
   burning their money in wastebaskets and listening
   to the Terror through the wall …

Summary and Explication: "Howl"

In its first line, "Howl" states that minds have been destroyed. In the following continuous stream of images, the poem addresses the mind and mental perception. Ginsberg's images describe gritty external city reality as well as inner psychic states. Much of Part I occurs in a city where the people he describes struggle to find their place. They are society's outcasts, homeless and jobless. The speaker witnesses social, political, and personal injustices that have the power to destroy people, or to destroy a person's mind. Many of the images seem grim, almost horrific, but the speaker belts them out with a joyous or angry enthusiasm. A lot of his vocabulary words—*angels, visionary, illuminated*—exalt the images.

The story of the publication of *Howl and Other Poems* is relevant to a poem expressing social outrage. When the small book, introduced by William Carlos Williams, was published in 1956 by City Lights Books, *Howl* was declared obscene for its lewd sexual content. Copies were confiscated, and its publisher, the poet Lawrence Ferlinghetti, was arrested. However, a judge decided that, in spite of its vulgar language, *Howl* had social importance and therefore could not be banned from sale. Ferlinghetti won his case. *Howl* went back on the bookshelves. Nearly a million copies of *Howl and Other Poems* have been sold. The book is still in print today and has been translated into twenty-two languages. Such enormous success for a book of poetry is highly unusual.

Poetic Technique

Ginsberg's "Howl" is 3,600 words and 112 lines long. He begins "Howl" with the words "I saw" but does not use "I" again until

Part II. He also does not use a period until the end of that very long Part I. The speaker, a visionary, lists what he sees in an intense collage of images. The poem sounds improvisational, like free association. Long lists of images begin with repetitions of "Moloch," in Part II, a Hebrew name of a god to whom children are sacrificed, and "I'm with you in Rockland," in Part III. Ginsberg's long lines did not sound like prose. He included poetic language and imagery in each line.[1]

The poem is somewhat surreal. There is a mix of the real and the unreal. Ginsberg did not use common verbs like walk, say, or think. Instead, people "dragged themselves" and "cowered" and "bared their brains." His word choices and word changes made creative images that seemed unreal. Ginsberg's images can start with a real incident. By changing a few words, he makes an image unreal or dreamlike, created in the mind. For example, the line, "expelled from the academies for crazy & publishing obscene odes on the windows of the skull," refers to a real incident. Ginsberg did get caught writing graffiti in college at Columbia. Rather than write, "windows on a building," however, he wrote "windows of the skull." The incident stayed with him in his mind.[2] And, as the first line says, the poem happens in the mind.

Themes

In "Howl," Ginsberg "howled" to express the frustration of a generation—young people looking for meaningful lives, free from repression. He merges his personal experiences with social commentary. In his poems, Ginsberg often contrasts urban cities with nature, and he protests the destruction of nature by industry. He speaks for a generation of people who felt torn between a desire

FACTS

The Beat Generation

In the 1950s, Jack Kerouac (1922–1969) coined the phrase "Beat Generation." It started as a small group of writers, friends of Ginsberg and Kerouac and William Burroughs. Kerouac's *On the Road* (1957) is a major work of the Beat Generation. Lawrence Ferlinghetti (1919–) cofounded City Lights Booksellers and Publishers, in San Francisco. The place is called Beat poetry's "literary headquarters." One of his most popular books is *A Coney Island of the Mind* (1958).

The Beat movement spread to Los Angeles, San Francisco, and New York City. Its artists and writers, called "Beatniks," lived "bohemian" lifestyles, meaning free and unconventional. They did not want to follow traditional rules of society. Beatniks promoted free expression as well as sexual and spiritual liberation. They wanted freedom from censorship and repression. They opposed the Vietnam War and led antiwar protests. They inspired the hippies of the 1960s and influenced musicians like Bob Dylan and the Beatles.

for complete freedom and an increasing pressure to succeed through education and industry. Ginsberg strove for spiritual peace over monetary success.

Ginsberg's Poetic Style

Ginsberg wrote poetry to express his ideas about society. He wrote about subjects that affected him personally, like his mother's mental illness and his homosexuality. Ginsberg wanted to break out of the limitations on subject matter. He wanted to express himself more freely. His poems were expressive, explosive, angry, and sexual. Ginsberg wrote expansive, spontaneous poems with long lines and long sentences. Ginsberg's style is similar to that of one of his favorite poets, Walt Whitman. Many of Ginsberg's poems are emotional and highly charged.

Howl made Ginsberg a well-known poet. The famous and sensational trial over the publication of *Howl* made him a political activist. Ginsberg endorsed First Amendment rights. He became a spokesperson for the Beat Generation.

In back of the real

railroad yard in San Jose
   I wandered desolate
in front of a tank factory
   and sat on a bench
near the switchman's shack.

A flower lay on the hay on
   the asphalt highway
—the dread hay flower
   I thought—It had a
brittle black stem and
   corolla of yellowish dirty
spikes like Jesus' inchlong
   crown, and a soiled
dry center cotton tuft
   like a used shaving brush
that's been lying under
   the garage for a year.

Yellow, yellow flower, and
   flower of industry,
tough spiky ugly flower,
   flower nonetheless,
with the form of the great yellow
   Rose in your brain!
This is the flower of the World.

Discussion

The poem's title is also its first line. Notice how much attention Ginsberg pays to a little flower behind a factory. In the midst of industry, nature blooms but it is also destroyed. The flower is cut and no longer living. It is an ordinary flower that might have gone unnoticed. Ginsberg gives it a lot of importance, however. As he focuses on the flower, he describes the rest of the surroundings.

What scene do you envision when you read the poem? How does the speaker's mood influence the scene? If Ginsberg used the flower as a symbol, what do you think it represents? What clues from the poem support your interpretation?

Uptown

Yellow-lit Budweiser signs over oaken bars,
"I've seen everything"—the bartender handing me change of $10,
I stared at him amiably eyes thru an obvious Adamic beard—
with Montana musicians homeless in Manhattan, teenage
curly hair themselves—we sat at the antique booth and gossiped,
Madame Grady's literary salon a curious value in New York—
"If I had my way I'd cut off your hair and send you to Vietnam"—
"Bless you then" I replied to a hated thin citizen hurrying to the
*   barroom door*
upon wet dark Amsterdam Avenue decades later—
"And if I couldn't do that I'd cut your throat" he snarled farewell,
and "Bless you sir" I added as he went to his fate in the rain, dapper
*   Irishman.*

Discussion

Many of Ginsberg's poems take place on gritty streets in cities where lots of people intermingle to live and gather, work and play. Tensions run high in this poem because of the "generation gap" combined with differing political ideas.

What is the speaker's attitude toward the "dapper Irishman"?

The poem is one long sentence. How does it sound when read aloud?

Major Works by ALLen Ginsberg

Howl and Other Poems (1956)

Kaddish and Other Poems (1961)

Reality Sandwiches (1963)

The Yage Letters (with William S. Burroughs, 1963)

Planet News (1968)

First Blues: Rags, Ballads & Harmonium Songs 1971–1974 (1975)

The Gates of Wrath: Rhymed Poems 1948–1951 (1972)

The Fall of America: Poems of These States (1973)

Iron Horse (1972)

Mind Breaths (1978)

Plutonian Ode: Poems 1977–1980 (1982)

Collected Poems: 1947–1980 (1984)

White Shroud Poems: 1980–1985 (1986)

Cosmopolitan Greetings Poems: 1986–1993 (1994)

Howl Annotated (1995)

Illuminated Poems (1996)

Selected Poems: 1947–1995 (1996)

Death and Fame: Poems 1993–1997 (1999)

Ginsberg with the Russian poet Yevgeni Yevtushenko (center) and Lawrence Ferlinghetti, the publisher of *Howl*.

ReLaTed PoeTS

Gary Snyder (1930–), author of *Riprap and Cold Mountain Poems* (1965), writes about nature and wilderness as well as Zen Buddhism. Snyder does not consider himself a Beat poet, but he was one of the six poets who read at the famous Six Gallery poetry reading.

Several teachers at Black Mountain College, North Carolina (an experimental college now defunct), were related to the Beat Movement. They are called the Black Mountain Poets and include Robert Creeley, Robert Duncan, Denise Levertov, and Charles Olson.

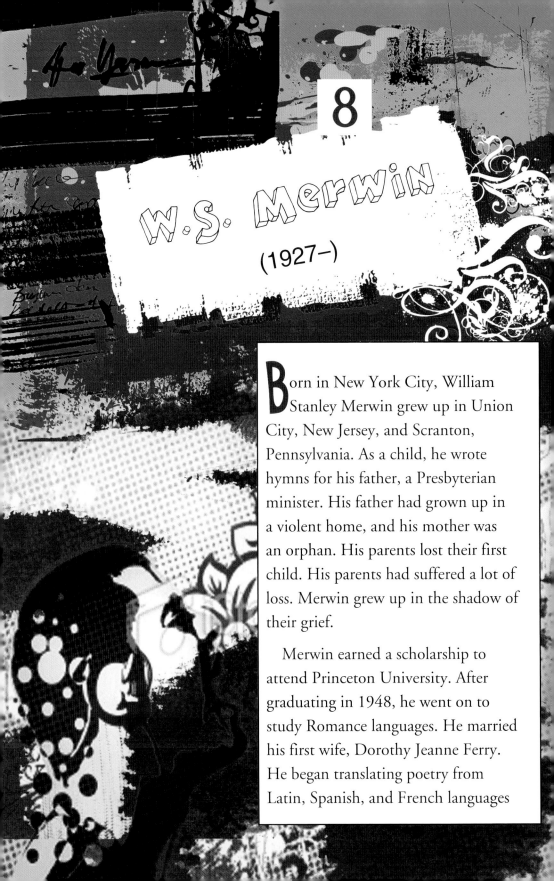

W.S. Merwin

(1927–)

Born in New York City, William Stanley Merwin grew up in Union City, New Jersey, and Scranton, Pennsylvania. As a child, he wrote hymns for his father, a Presbyterian minister. His father had grown up in a violent home, and his mother was an orphan. His parents lost their first child. His parents had suffered a lot of loss. Merwin grew up in the shadow of their grief.

Merwin earned a scholarship to attend Princeton University. After graduating in 1948, he went on to study Romance languages. He married his first wife, Dorothy Jeanne Ferry. He began translating poetry from Latin, Spanish, and French languages

W. S. Merwin

into English. Translation work helped him understand the language of poetry. He also tutored children of wealthy families. In 1950, he got a tutoring job in Majorca, Spain. While he was in Europe, living in Spain, England, and France, he met Dido Milroy, a woman fifteen years his senior. She helped him find translation work and introduced him to literary figures. His first book of poetry, *A Mask for Janus*, was chosen in 1952 by W. H. Auden for the Yale Series of Younger Poets.

Merwin returned to the United States in 1956 to accept a fellowship to write plays for a theater company in Cambridge, Massachusetts. His first marriage ended and he married Milroy, the woman he met in Europe. In Cambridge, he met Robert Lowell, Sylvia Plath, and other poets. He decided to focus more on poetry and less on plays.

Merwin moved back to Europe and lived in London and the south of France. He spent time with Sylvia Plath and her husband, Ted Hughes. He saw the couple's marital problems and grieved when Plath committed suicide. Merwin and Milroy separated in 1968.

In 1970, Merwin published *The Carrier of Ladders*, a book that earned the 1971 Pulitzer Prize for Poetry. He donated his thousand-dollar prize to an organization that opposed the Vietnam War. In 1976, Merwin moved to Maui, Hawaii, to study with a Zen Buddhist master. Merwin married his third wife, Paula Schwartz, in a Buddhist ceremony in 1983. The couple lived in a house Merwin helped to design. Merwin, whose Buddhist, pacifist, and environmental beliefs influenced his writing, restored his property's eroded land by planting endangered trees and plants.

Unlike many of his contemporaries, Merwin did not pursue a teaching career. He has published over twenty books of poetry and twenty books of translation, plays, and memoirs. He has won many prizes and honors. He was a Chancellor of the Academy of American Poets. Along with Rita Dove and Louise Glück, Merwin served as U.S. Poet Laureate Consultant for the bicentennial year of the Library of Congress in 2000. He lives and works in Hawaii.

FACTS

Recent Poet Laureates

Donald Hall (1928–) served as the U.S. poet laureate from 2006 to 2007. When Billy Collins reviewed Hall's *Selected Poems* for the *Washington Post*, he wrote, "Hall has long been placed in the Frostian tradition of the plainspoken rural poet."[1] Collins praised Hall for his engaging simplicity. Ted Kooser (1939–) served as the U.S. Poet Laureate from 2004 to 2006. He taught at the University of Nebraska-Lincoln. Like Collins, Kooser also strives for clarity in his poems. Other recent poet laureates include Louise Glück, Stanley Kunitz, Robert Pinsky, Robert Hass, Rita Dove, and Charles Simic.

For the Anniversary of My Death

Every year without knowing it I have passed the day
When the last fires will wave to me
And the silence will set out
Tireless traveler
Like the beam of a lightless star

Then I will no longer
Find myself in life as in a strange garment
Surprised at the earth
And the love of one woman
And the shamelessness of men
As today writing after three days of rain
Hearing the wren sing and the falling cease
And bowing not knowing to what

Summary and Explication: "For The Anniversary of My Death"

In this short, compact poem, Merwin is able to speak rather calmly about his own death and other mysteries. He sounds as comfortable with death as he is with life. He calls his body "a strange garment" and is "surprised" at the earth. His last line reveals that he has faith, though he is not sure what to believe in. Rather than being uncomfortable with this state of unknowing, however, he simply wonders about life and death in this poem. By the end, he returns to a specific day—today—and to ordinary daily life.

Poetic Technique

"For the Anniversary of My Death" is short. The poem is not set in a specific place or time. It is not punctuated. Its language is simple and clear. However, the poem quickly takes the reader to an unclear, mysterious realm. After his somewhat alarming first line (many people have not considered that they unknowingly "celebrate" a calendar day that will be the opposite of a birthday), Merwin enters the unknown. He describes death using abstract symbolic language, in terms of "last fires" and "silence."

Themes

Many of Merwin's poems address the unknown. They describe an almost surreal state of unknowingness, a mysterious nothingness, a void perhaps. He writes about themes of life and death in a way that is both basic and spiritual. In "For the Anniversary of My Death," Merwin is able to confront the reality of his death and then return to happy, ordinary daily life. Rain ends and birds sing; they are such peaceful images. After confronting death, Merwin manages to end the poem with the comforts of daily life and with a note of faith.

Merwin's Poetic Style

Merwin's first book, *A Mask for Janus* (1952), was chosen in 1952 by W. H. Auden for the Yale Series of Younger Poets Prize. Auden liked that Merwin's poems were formal and expertly crafted. When Merwin wrote the book, he had been translating medieval poetry. Inspired by his work as a translator, he used classical imagery and myth in his poems.

Two of his next books, *Green with Beasts* (1956) and *The Drunk in the Furnace* (1960), showed a shift in poetic style, one he would hone in his later work. After Merwin met Robert Lowell, he began using plain American language. He experimented with the way his poems looked. He stopped using punctuation. He stopped using traditional meter. He wrote open, "disordered" poems.[2] He developed an introspective style and wrote about personal subjects. He used his new style to write *The Lice* (1967) and *The Carrier of Ladders* (1970). They are thought to be his best and most influential books. He won a Pulitzer Prize for *The Carriers of Ladders.* He won another Pulitzer Prize in 2009 for his book *The Shadow of Sirius.*

Merwin has the ability to speak in an intimate voice that is not too personal. He has been called a visionary.[3] He writes abstract poems about the experience of silence, death, nothingness, the unknown, and life's deep mysteries. Many of his poems describe psychological states. Because his images do not always seem connected, his poems often seem surreal, with no narrative story and no sense of time or place.

The Flight

At times in the day
I thought of a fire to watch
not that my hands were cold
but to have that doorway to see through
into the first thing
even our names are made of fire
and we feed on night
walking I thought of a fire
turning around I caught sight of it
in an opening in the wall
in another house and another
before and after
in house after house that was mine to see
the same fire the perpetual bird

Discussion

The images in "The Flight" do not seem to refer to anything concrete. The nouns are simple—flight, fire, night, and cold. He captures an inner experience, one that is hard to articulate, in words. What feeling does Merwin convey in the poem? Though the poem has no punctuation, what punctuation is implied by the words?

Late Wonders

In Los Angeles the cars are flowing
through the white air
and the news of bombings
at Universal Studios
you can ride through an avalanche
if you have never
ridden through an avalanche

with your ticket
you can ride on a trolley
before which the Red
Sea parts
just the way it did
for Moses

you can see Los Angeles
destroyed hourly
you can watch the avenue named for somewhere else
the one on which you know you are
crumple and vanish incandescent
with a terrible cry
all around you
rising from the houses and families of everyone you
have seen all day
driving shopping talking eating

it's only a movie
it's only a beam of light

Discussion

"Late Wonders," unlike many of Merwin's poems, has a more concrete story. It is located in a real setting but the Hollywood movie set has a sense of the unreal. What purpose does the Hollywood setting serve in the poem? What is the message of this poem?

Major Works by W. S. Merwin

Poetry

A Mask for Janus (1952)

Green with Beasts (1956)

The Drunk in the Furnace (1960)

The Lice (1967)

The Carrier of Ladders (1970)

The Compass Flower (1977)

Opening the Hand (1983)

The Rain in the Trees (1988)

Travels (1993)

The Vixen (1996)

Flower and Hand: Poems 1977–1983 (1997)

The River Sound (1999)

The Pupil (2002)

Migration: New & Selected Poems (2005)

Present Company (2007)

Prose

The Lost Upland (1992)

Summer Doorways (2006)

The Book of Fables (2007)

Related Poets

Galway Kinnell, a classmate of Merwin's at Princeton, is the author of *The Book of Nightmares* and other books. John Berryman, Merwin's teaching assistant in a college class, wrote *77 Dream Songs*.

9

SYLVIA PLATH

(1932–1963)

Sylvia Plath grew up on the Massachusetts coast where her parents both taught school. Her strict, German-immigrant father taught biology and specialized in bees. He died when Plath was eight years old. Plath's family, including her maternal Austrian grandparents, moved to Wellesley, Massachusetts, outside Boston. Her mother taught high school to support Plath and her younger brother, Warren.[1]

In school, Plath was bright and high achieving. In high school, she published short stories and poems. She earned a fellowship to attend Smith, the women's college in Northampton, Massachusetts. In college, she won

Sylvia Plath

prizes for stories she published in *Mademoiselle* and *Seventeen* magazines. In June 1953, she won an internship as guest editor of *Mademoiselle* magazine for one month in New York City. She stayed with other interns at a nearby hotel.

She returned home, exhausted. She had hoped to spend the rest of the summer in a Harvard writing class, but her application was rejected. She fell into a depression. She tried to commit suicide. She was treated with psychotherapy and electroshock therapy. Plath missed a year of college due to her illness, but she still graduated from Smith with honors in 1954. She later wrote her novel, *The Bell Jar*, based on her internship. Like Plath, the book's main character studied at Smith, worked as a magazine editor, and suffered a nervous breakdown.

In 1955, she studied at Cambridge University in England on a Fulbright Fellowship. One night at a party she met a British poet she admired named Ted Hughes. Only four months later, she married him. The couple moved back to Massachusetts. Plath wanted to focus on writing, but to earn money she taught freshman English at her alma mater, Smith. She also took a writing class taught by Robert Lowell. One of her classmates was Anne Sexton, who would also go on to publish many books of poetry. Plath also met W. S. Merwin, who became a good friend.

Plath became pregnant in 1959, so she and Hughes returned to England. They had two children, a girl and a boy. Between the births of her children, Plath suffered a miscarriage. After the experience of pregnancy and motherhood, Plath had an outpouring of creativity and wrote many poems expressing the full gamut of her emotions, from joy to grief.

In 1961, Plath published her first book of poems, *Colossus.* Plath was devastated, in 1962, to discover that her husband was having an affair. She asked him to move out. She took her children to a new apartment in London. That winter in London was one of the coldest on record. The apartment had no phone and little heat. The children were sick. Though Hughes visited the children, Plath was alone with few friends near. She grew severely depressed.

Plath wrote twelve new poems in just two weeks in the chilly London flat. In January 1963, her semiautobiographical novel *The Bell Jar* was published under the pen name Victoria Lucas. At age thirty, on February 11, 1963, Plath made sure her children were safe and had food, sealed herself in the kitchen, and turned on the

FACTS

Plath at Cambridge

After graduating with highest honors from Smith College, Plath earned a Fulbright scholarship to study at Newnham College at Cambridge University. The cobblestone streets of Cambridge are lined with shops and cafés. The campus has courtyards, gardens, and paths along the River Cam. At the time, Newnham students wore black robes to class.

According to author Anne Stevenson, Plath

> had come to Cambridge with a new set of white and gold Samsonite luggage, together with a bicycle she had imported, and was often seen pedaling furiously around the town, her black gown billowing out behind like an undisciplined shadow.[2]

Plath's time in England changed her life. There, she met the man she married, the poet Ted Hughes. She spent the last years of her life in London, where she wrote some of her best work.

gas oven. Two years after her suicide, her book of poems *Ariel* was published. Her poetry became extremely popular. In 1982, she became the first poet to win a posthumous Pulitzer Prize, for her *Collected Poems*.

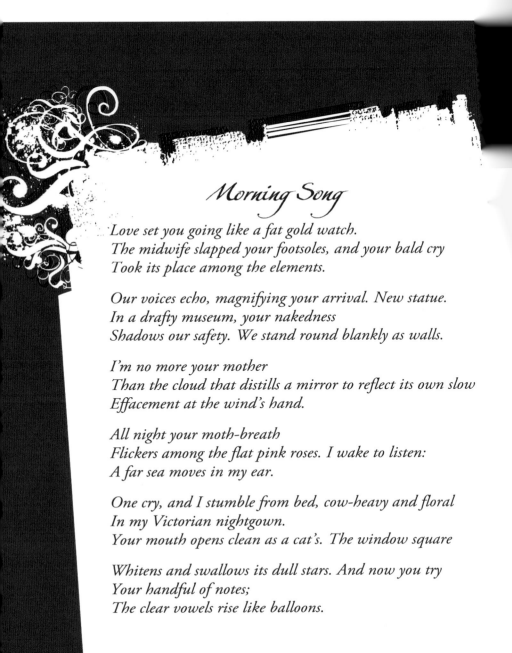

Morning Song

Love set you going like a fat gold watch.
The midwife slapped your footsoles, and your bald cry
Took its place among the elements.

Our voices echo, magnifying your arrival. New statue.
In a drafty museum, your nakedness
Shadows our safety. We stand round blankly as walls.

I'm no more your mother
Than the cloud that distills a mirror to reflect its own slow
Effacement at the wind's hand.

All night your moth-breath
Flickers among the flat pink roses. I wake to listen:
A far sea moves in my ear.

One cry, and I stumble from bed, cow-heavy and floral
In my Victorian nightgown.
Your mouth opens clean as a cat's. The window square

Whitens and swallows its dull stars. And now you try
Your handful of notes;
The clear vowels rise like balloons.

Summary and ExpLicaTion: "Morning Song"

The speaker in the poem is a new mother. She has just delivered a baby. She does not sound serene or peaceful, however. Delivering a child is exhausting and emotional. The new baby is now separate from the mother. She describes the child as a "fat gold watch." The image is precise and mechanical. It focuses on time—a lifetime. A human life has begun. The baby's "nakedness," its vulnerability, "shadows our safety." Her role and her self-identity have changed. Her senses are heightened, focused on the child.

PoeTic Technique

Plath's language is crisp and precise. Her language is like her own line in the poem, "clean as a cat's." As she wrote, Plath spoke her poems aloud to herself so she could hear their sound. If you read this poem aloud, you can hear how the vowels and consonants interconnect; there are lots of *s* and *c* sounds.

"Morning Song" is full of bright, joyful images and similes, but there is an emotional intensity of distance or fear. In the first line, Plath says the baby is "like a fat gold watch." This short brilliant simile is rich in meaning. The watch symbolizes a lifetime; a baby begins to age from the moment of birth. The image may also reveal the speaker's fear of the child. Plath's first visual image is of an expensive, beautiful *thing*, a mechanical device, not something usually associated with a newborn baby.

Similes provide layers of meaning to poetry because they often do not mean only one thing. For example, how do you interpret the line, "We stand round blankly as walls"? What could Plath mean by comparing herself to a wall?

Themes

Plath wrote intense, emotional, personal poems. Plath wrote a lot about her relationship with her father. The bee imagery she uses in several poems may come from the fact that her father was a bee specialist. History fascinated her. She was a brilliant researcher. She used images of the Holocaust and other historical references.

She wrote about sexuality, death, and mental illness. She wrote poems while she was immersed in her marriage and raising her children. Being a wife and mother shaped her identity, but it also conflicted with her identity as a writer. Motherhood inspired Sylvia Plath's fierce streak of creativity. She quickly wrote many poems after the birth of her children. The linguistically brilliant poems are emotionally charged and address intense conflicts of the joys and challenges of motherhood.

Plath's Poetic Style

At the time of Plath's death, she had entered an exciting phase in her writing. Her old poems, the poems in *Colossus*, seemed safe compared to her new work. The poems that would appear in *Ariel* felt brilliantly alive. They were so emotionally charged that she read them aloud as she wrote. She precisely placed every word, like links in a chain, so her lines would crackle with energy and force.

In *Life Studies*, Robert Lowell wrote about his own life in a confessional way. Plath loved the book. Plath also admired her classmate and friend Anne Sexton. Sexton's poems about motherhood and about nervous breakdowns had a new psychological depth. Plath began to freely write about her own mental illness, personal troubles, and sexuality.[3]

In some of Plath's poems there is a contrast between her language and her tone. She can describe violent imagery with a childlike tone. Some of her dark, lyric poems almost sound like nursery rhymes. She wrote frankly about her own life, about topics like motherhood, depression, and marriage. She did not live to appreciate the enormous public applause that *Ariel* received.

Sylvia Plath with her mother and children. Many of her poems dealt with motherhood.

The Couriers

The word of a snail on the plate of a leaf?
It is not mine. Do not accept it.

Acetic acid in a sealed tin?
Do not accept it. It is not genuine.

A ring of gold with the sun in it?
Lies. Lies and a grief.

Frost on a leaf, the immaculate
Cauldron, talking and crackling

All to itself on the top of each
Of nine black Alps,

A disturbance in mirrors,
The sea shattering its grey one—

Love, love, my season.

Discussion

"The Couriers" is the second poem in *Ariel,* right after "Morning Song." The couriers, or messengers, in the poem are all natural elements. The first three couplets, in question and answer format, list three denials of one of nature's messages.

How is the poem resolved in the final three couplets and last line? How does Plath use crisp language and internal rhyme in "The Couriers"?

Mirror

I am silver and exact. I have no preconceptions.
Whatever I see I swallow immediately
Just as it is, unmisted by love or dislike.
I am not cruel, only truthful —
The eye of a little god, four-cornered.
Most of the time I meditate on the opposite wall.
It is pink, with speckles. I have looked at it so long
I think it is a part of my heart. But it flickers.
Faces and darkness separate us over and over.
Now I am a lake. A woman bends over me,
Searching my reaches for what she really is.
Then she turns to those liars, the candles or the moon.
I see her back, and reflect it faithfully.
She rewards me with tears and an agitation of hands.
I am important to her. She comes and goes.
Each morning it is her face that replaces the darkness.
In me she has drowned a young girl, and in me an old woman
Rises toward her day after day, like a terrible fish.

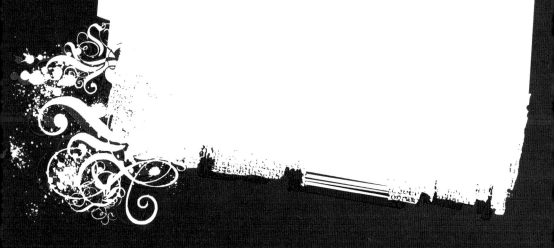

Discussion

The speaker of "Mirror" is the mirror. The mirror describes a woman who looks into it.

What does the mirror see? How does the mirror describe the woman looking into it? What emotional state does Plath describe?

Major Works by Sylvia Plath

Poetry

The Colossus (1960)
Ariel (1965)
Crossing the Water (1971)
Winter Trees (1972)
The Collected Poems (1981)

Prose

The Bell Jar (1963)
Letters Home (1975, to and edited by her mother)
Johnny Panic and the Bible of Dreams (1977)
The Journals of Sylvia Plath (1982)
The Unabridged Journals of Sylvia Plath (2000, edited by
    Karen V. Kukil)

Books for Young Readers

The Bed Book (1976)
The It-Doesn't-Matter-Suit (1996)
Collected Children's Stories (2001)
Mrs. Cherry's Kitchen (2001)

ReLaTed PoeTs

Sylvia Plath's friend Anne Sexton wrote poems about her experience as a woman. Some of her poems, like Plath's, are emotional personal accounts of marriage and motherhood, birth and death. Plath's husband was the poet Ted Hughes. Try his book *Crow*.

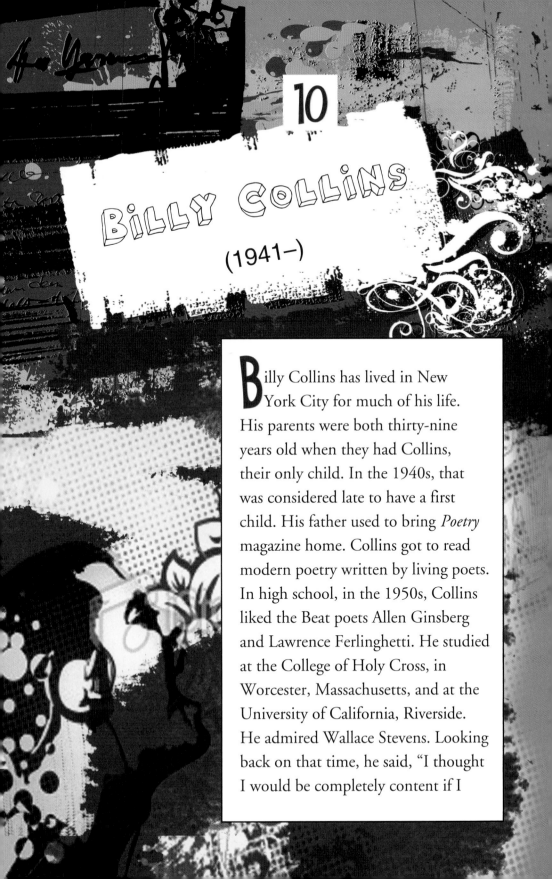

BiLLY COLLiNS

(1941–)

Billy Collins has lived in New York City for much of his life. His parents were both thirty-nine years old when they had Collins, their only child. In the 1940s, that was considered late to have a first child. His father used to bring *Poetry* magazine home. Collins got to read modern poetry written by living poets. In high school, in the 1950s, Collins liked the Beat poets Allen Ginsberg and Lawrence Ferlinghetti. He studied at the College of Holy Cross, in Worcester, Massachusetts, and at the University of California, Riverside. He admired Wallace Stevens. Looking back on that time, he said, "I thought I would be completely content if I

Billy Collins

was recognized at some later point in my life as a third-rate Wallace Stevens."[1]

In 1968, Collins began teaching English at Lehman College, City University of New York. He is now a distinguished professor. Collins has conducted summer poetry workshops in Ireland at University College Galway. He also taught at Columbia University and was a writer-in-residence at Sarah Lawrence College.

After he published his first book of poems, Collins quickly began winning awards and gaining a wide popular appeal. In 2001, he was named U.S. poet laureate. He served for two years. In 2002, Collins appeared on Garrison Keillor's popular radio show *A Prairie Home Companion.* His popularity soared. In 2004, he became New York's State Poet.

FACTS

Collins Interview

Some of the information for this chapter was taken from "A Brisk Walk: Billy Collins in Conversation." If you want to read the entire interview, log on to the Web site of the Academy of American Poets and find the page about Billy Collins.

Boy Shooting at a Statue

It was late afternoon,
the beginning of winter, a light snow,
and I was the only one in the park

to witness the lone boy running
in circles around the base of a bronze statue.
I could not read the carved name

of the statesman who loomed above,
one hand on his cold hip,
but as the boy ran, head down,

he would point a finger at the statue
and pull an imaginary trigger
imitating the sounds of rapid gunfire.

Evening thickened, the mercury sank,
but the boy kept running in the circle
of his footprints in the snow

shooting blindly into the air.
History will never find a way to end,
I thought, as I left the park by the north gate

and walked slowly home
returning to the station of my desk
where the sheets of paper I wrote on

were like pieces of glass
through which I could see
hundreds of dark birds circling in the sky below.

Summary and Explication: "Boy Shooting at a Statue"

In a park, the speaker watches a boy pretend to shoot a statue with his imaginary finger-gun. The statue cannot respond, of course. The statue is a representation of an unnamed person, honored for his role in history. The boy, immersed in his game, is unaware that the speaker is watching. He runs around the statue. He repeats his actions. From his observations, the speaker makes the sweeping statement that "History will never end." The speaker returns home and sits at his desk. He looks at his writing paper and seems to have a vision.

Poetic Technique

In this poem of three-line stanzas, Collins has a gentle humor. For example, in line 3 he says, "I was the only one in the park …" He is not alone at all, however. With the timing of a comedian, he pauses with a line break and a stanza break before admitting there was also a little boy in the park. He means he was the only one to see the boy playing. As he develops the poem, he connects the narrative, the story of the boy playing, to a personal reflection. He tries to get meaning from the image of the boy in the park.

Themes

The scene is comical, but it also has a sense of loneliness. The first stanza establishes time and place. It is winter, snowing, growing colder, and getting dark. The images suggest sadness and solitude. The speaker makes it sound as if by watching the boy play he is witnessing some kind of historic event.

Collins likes his poems to move from a simple story to a profound ending. He likes to surprise the reader in the middle of a poem. He likes the beginnings to be simple, common, and easily understood. "Boy Shooting at a Statue" ends when the speaker has a somewhat surreal vision. Looking into a piece of paper, as if paper were glass, he sees "hundreds of dark birds circling in the sky below." The speaker's vision has something to do with the boy in the park and with his belief about history. The poem ends just as the speaker is about to try to create something from the experience. The poem ends as the speaker begins to write a poem. What feeling do you get from Collins's final image?

Collins's Poetic Style

Billy Collins has earned both critical praise and a wide readership. He has an enormous popularity that is rare for a poet. Readers enjoy his clear, straightforward poems. Collins uses a friendly tone and has a dry, gentle humor, but he also makes profound statements. He says that he likes to start out with an ordinary scene and surprise the reader by leading the poem to a strange twist.

Some of his humorous poems poke fun at poetry that is intense and difficult, like the kind he once tried to write. Collins even takes potshots at poetry he loves. One of his books is entitled *The Trouble with Poetry*. He makes fun of poetry that is pretentious, or too full of itself. Collins has recognized that poetry does not have a wide readership in the United States. One reason may be that it is too obscure. Collins himself started out trying to write difficult poems. The turning point came when he realized that "Clarity is the real risk in poetry because you are exposed."[2]

Collins often blends humor with contrasting emotions such as grief, longing, and sadness. He writes humorously about painful

Collins at a poetry reading in California

topics like loss and death. Those poems allow readers to gently laugh at their own fears and troubles.

Collins uses a consistent voice, as if it is the same guy speaking in every poem. He defines *voice* as a way to "invent this one character who resembles you, obviously, and probably is more like you than anyone else on earth, but is not the equivalent to you."[3] He likes a reader to feel as if a poem's speaker is talking directly to him or her.

Collins's poetry has gained a huge mass-market audience. In a time when many contemporary poets are overlooked and struggle to make a living, Collins is as well known as a blockbuster novelist, and he makes about as much money, an extraordinarily rare thing in the world of poetry.

Special Glasses

I had to send away for them
because they are not available in any store.

They look the same as any sunglasses
with a light tint and silvery frames,
but instead of filtering out the harmful
rays of the sun,

they filter out the harmful sight of you —
you on the approach,
you waiting at my bus stop,
you, face in the evening window.

Every morning I put them on
and step out the side door
whistling a melody of thanks to my nose
and my ears for holding them in place, just so,

singing a song of gratitude
to the lens grinder at his heavy bench
and to the very lenses themselves
because they allow it all to come in, all but you.

How they know the difference
between the green hedges, the stone walls,
and you is beyond me,

yet the schoolbuses flashing in the rain
do come in, as well as the postman waving
and the mother and daughter dogs next door,

and then there is the tea kettle
about to play its chord –
everything sailing right in but you, girl.

Yes, just as the night air passes through the screen,
but not the mosquito,
and as water swirls down the drain,
but not the eggshell,
so the flowering trellis and the moon
pass through my special glasses, but not you.

Let us keep it this way, I say to myself,
as I lay my special glasses on the night table,
pull the chain on the lamp,
and say a prayer—unlike the song—
that I will not see you in my dreams.

Discussion

The speaker needs "special glasses" to avoid seeing a certain girl. Notice Collins's use of dry, understated humor. With a straight-faced, deadpan tone, Collins suggests the fantastical and hilarious idea that a store might sell glasses that would blot out only one person.

The speaker addresses the girl but does not tell us anything about her or his relationship to her. Who is she? Who is the speaker? What clues help you figure out who they are?

Does it matter that we do not know anything about these people? If yes, why? If no, what is the poem about?

The Student

My poetry instruction book,
which I bought at an outdoor stall along the river,

contains many rules
about what to avoid and what to follow.

More than two people in a poem
is a crowd, is one.

Mention what clothes you are wearing
as you compose, is another.

Avoid the word vortex,
the word velvety, and the word cicada.

When at a loss for an ending,
have some brown hens standing in the rain.

Never admit that you revise.
And—always keep your poem in one season.

I try to be mindful,
but in these last days of summer

whenever I look up from my page
and see a burn-mark of yellow leaves,

I think of the icy winds
that will soon be knifing through my jacket.

Discussion

Collins's poem gently mocks the world of poetry. It is a poem about the rules of writing a poem. Even as the speaker tries diligently to follow the rules, he ultimately breaks them. The speaker worries that his threatened comfort will distract him from the poetry rules. Collins seems to gently mock himself and the human condition.

Do you think there should be rules for writing poetry? What do you think Collins thinks about rules for poetry?

Major Works by BiLLy CoLLiNS

Pokerface (1977)
Video Poems (1980)
The Apple That Astonished Paris (1988)
Questions About Angels (1991)
The Art of Drowning (1995)
Picnic, Lightning (1998)
Sailing Alone Around the Room: New and Selected Poems (2001)
Nine Horses (2002)
The Trouble with Poetry (2005)
Ballistics (2008)

Related Poets

If you enjoy humorous poems, you might like James Tate, Charles Simic, and Kenneth Koch.

Louise Glück

(1943–)

Louise Glück (pronounced GLICK) was born in New York City and grew up on Long Island. She loved to read and was encouraged by her parents who, she wrote, "admired intellectual accomplishment."[1] In high school, she battled anorexia, an illness she later wrote about in her poetry. In 1961, after she graduated from Hewlett High School, she spent several years in psychoanalysis. Her therapy also inspired her writing. She said, "The impulses that produced anorexia as a symptom are evident in my work. Do I write about anorexia? Rarely and only once directly."[2]

She went on to study at Sarah Lawrence College and Columbia

Louise Glück

University. For a time, she did not think of writing as a career. She earned a degree from Williams College, in Williamstown, Massachusetts. She married, had a son, and got divorced. For several years, Glück taught at different schools as a visiting writer and poet-in-residence. She published her book, *First Born*, in 1968. It began her steady and successful career as a published poet.

In 1983, Glück joined the permanent faculty at Williams College. She held that teaching position for twenty years, until 2004. In 1993, she earned a Pulitzer Prize for her book *The Wild Iris.* She served as Vermont State Poet from 1994 to 1998.

Glück is a private person. She tries to stay out of the public eye. She does not like to be photographed. For her, being an artist is public enough. She believes an artist's work reveals a lot about a person, even if the information is not personal or factual.[3]

Even though she is shy of publicity, she gladly accepted the position of U.S. Poet Laureate in 2003, following Billy Collins. In 2004, she became writer-in-residence at Yale University and began to judge the prestigious Yale Series of Younger Poets. She enjoys cooking, working out in the gym, and reading detective novels.[4]

The Triumph of Achilles

In the story of Patroclus
no one survives, not even Achilles
who was nearly a god.
Patroclus resembled him; they wore
the same armor.

Always in these friendships
one serves the other, one is less than the other:
the hierarchy
is always apparent, though the legends
cannot be trusted —
their source is the survivor,
the one who has been abandoned.

What were the Greek ships on fire
compared to this loss?

In his tent, Achilles
grieved with his whole being
and the gods saw

he was a man already dead, a victim
of the part that loved,
the part that was mortal.

Summary and Explication: "The Triumph of Achilles"

"The Triumph of Achilles" tells a story from the epic poem *The Iliad* by the Greek poet Homer. During the Trojan War, the death of Patroclus set a significant chain of events in motion. "No one survives," writes Glück. The story is that Achilles fought with the Greek army against Troy. Prince Hector, the brother of Paris (who abducted Helen), fought for Troy. The two were enemies. Patroclus, Achilles' close friend and student, wore Achilles' armor into battle one day. Believing Patroclus was Achilles, Hector killed him. In rage and grief, Achilles killed Hector. In turn, a skilled Trojan archer shot Achilles in the one place he was vulnerable to attack, his heel.

Poetic Technique

Glück uses short lines and clear specific language. The poem is written from a third-person omniscient (or all-knowing) point of view. She often creates a serious tone. Her humor is often understated irony. The title itself is somewhat ironic. How could pain, loss, and death be a triumph for Achilles? In what way does Achilles triumph? Perhaps Glück suggests that what makes a human most vulnerable, and what is most painful, is a triumph.

Themes

Glück often wrote about loss and love. In "The Triumph of Achilles," Achilles' love for Patroclus led, perhaps, to both their deaths. Glück calls Achilles a "victim" of love; suggesting that love is a weakness. She says that "the gods saw" Achilles' situation (she refers to the mythic Greek gods). However, she does not say how the gods responded or whether or not they intervened on his behalf (as they often do in Greek mythology). It might seem like a harsh perspective. In analyzing Glück's work, the poet Tony Hoagland wrote, "Though they appear ruthlessly truthful … the poems are often enough (not always) the flawed logic of a damaged speaker."[5]

When Glück refers to a myth, it helps to know the story, but it is not entirely necessary. In "The Triumph of Achilles," Glück uses myth to describe larger themes—friendship, love, and loss. Her poem offers a meaningful way to interpret the story of Achilles and Patroclus, but the other topic of the poem is about what it means to be human. In the second stanza, Glück departs from the myth and states a philosophy that can be applied to any friendship.

Glück's Poetic Style

Glück's poetry has been highly praised. She has received many awards. Many critics have exclaimed over the spare, economical quality of her intelligent poems. She has the ability to use simple language to discuss complex issues. Her poems are direct yet philosophical. They are clear and stark, yet lyrical and dramatic. Themes common in her poems are loss, rejection, isolation, and death, often specific to women.

Her haunting poems often create an ominous feeling. Her matter-of-fact tone can sound chilling when she speaks of dark, emotional events. One reason that her short poems are so powerful is that they address the mystery of the unknown. What is not said is as important as what is. In an essay in *Proofs & Theories: Essays on Poetry*, she wrote, "That which we do not know, of the universe, of mortality, is so much more vast than that which we do know. What is unfinished or has been destroyed participates in these mysteries. The problem is to make a whole that does not forfeit this power."[6]

Glück writes from her life experiences, but her poems are not necessarily autobiographical. She often uses myth to explore topics such as marriage, love, divorce, and family relationships. Each of Glück's books has its own unifying theme that links the poems. For example, in *The Wild Iris,* she uses the language of flowers. Flowers speak to the gardener. In *Averno,* she retells the myth of Persephone.

FACTS

The Myth of Persephone

In the myth, Hades, lord of the underworld, abducts Persephone to be his queen. Demeter, Persephone's mother and goddess of harvest, is grief stricken. She withdraws her fertility and Earth sinks into desolate winter. Hades agrees to let Persephone return to Earth. However, she must live with Hades every year for as many months as pomegranate seeds she ate in the underworld. When Persephone comes to Earth, it is spring. Her return to the underworld brings winter.

Glück presents a new take on this old story. Speaking in the voice of Persephone, Glück describes Hades as cavalier and suave. He tries to win Persephone by making her mother look bad. Not everyone would apply this specific interpretation to the myth.

A painting shows Hades returning Persephone to her mother,
Demeter, after her abduction to the underworld.

Pomegranate

First he gave me
his heart. It was
red fruit containing
many seeds, the skin
leathery, unlikely.
I preferred
to starve, bearing
out my training.
Then he said Behold
how the world looks, minding
your mother. I
peered under his arm:
What had she done
with color & odor?
Whereupon he said Now there
is a woman who loves
with a vengeance, adding
Consider she is in her element:
the trees turning to her, whole
villages going under
although in hell
the bushes are still
burning with pomegranates.
At which
he cut one open & began
to suck. When he looked up at last
it was to say My dear
you are your own
woman, finally, but examine
this grief your mother
parades over our heads
remembering
that she is one to whom
these depths were not offered.

Discussion

The single-word title, "Pomegranate," invokes the myth of Demeter (or Ceres) and Persephone (or Proserpine), mother and daughter. The small poem has an enormously rich story as its background. Glück does not mention names in the poem, but the mythic characters are recognizable.

The poem is told in the voice of Persephone. How would you describe her voice and her personality? What does Persephone's story add to the poem? How is the poem relevant beyond the myth? How can a reader identify with it?

Brown Circle

My mother wants to know
why, if I hate
family so much,
I went ahead and
had one. I don't
answer my mother.
What I hated
was being a child,
having no choice about
what people I loved.

I don't love my son
the way I meant to love him.
I thought I'd be
the lover of orchids who finds
red trillium growing
in the pine shade, and doesn't
touch it, doesn't need
to possess it. What I am
is the scientist,
who comes to that flower
with a magnifying glass
and doesn't leave, though
the sun burns a brown
circle of grass around
the flower. Which is
more or less the way
my mother loved me.

I must learn
to forgive my mother,
now that I am helpless
to spare my son.

Discussion

In her book *Ararat,* Glück wrote about her life, stripped of myth or metaphor. She still keeps her clean lines and simple language. This long, thin poem is written in the style of her earlier poems. However, it is a frank look at her real experience of being a mother.

Motherly attention, care, and love may damage her beloved son. The poem is personal. Now that Glück has become a mother, she sees her own mother in a new light. Her poem is not simple, however. "Brown Circle" does not end with sentimental forgiveness.

What is the emotional tone of the poem? How does Glück achieve the tone? How does Glück's speaker defy a typical image of motherhood?

Witchgrass

Something
comes into the world unwelcome
calling disorder, disorder—

If you hate me so much
don't bother to give me
a name: do you need
one more slur
in your language, another
way to blame
one tribe for everything—

as we both know,
if you worship
one god, you only need
one enemy—

I'm not the enemy.
Only a ruse to ignore
what you see happening
right here in this bed,
a little paradigm
of failure. One of your precious flowers
dies here almost every day
and you can't rest until
you attack the cause, meaning
whatever is left, whatever
happens to be sturdier
than your personal passion—

It was not meant
to last forever in the real world.
But why admit that, when you can go on
doing what you always do,
mourning and laying blame,
always the two together.

I don't need your praise
to survive. I was here first,
before you were here, before
you ever planted a garden.
And I'll be here when only the sun and moon
are left, and the sea, and the wide field.

I will constitute the field.

Discussion

Some of the poems in *The Wild Iris* are spoken in the voice of flowers. "Witchgrass" is told from the point of view of a persistent weed, one that is hard to get rid of. Most people do not like witchgrass.

What personality does Glück give the weed? How does this poem express anger about relationships?

Major Works by Louise Glück

Poetry

Firstborn (1968)
The House on Marshland (1975)
The Garden (1976)
Descending Figure (1980)
The Triumph of Achilles (1985)
Ararat (1990)
The Wild Iris (1992)
The First Four Books of Poems (1995)
Meadowlands (1996)
Vita Nova (1999)
The Seven Ages (2001)

Prose

Proofs and Theories: Essays on Poetry (1994)

Related Poets

Glück's teacher was the poet Stanley Kunitz. Other Vermont State poets are Ellen Bryant Voigt (1943–), Grace Paley (1922–2007), and Ruth Stone (1915–). If you like Louise Glück, you might enjoy Carolyn Forché (1950–) and Mary Oliver (1935–). You might also like Jorie Graham (1950–), especially her first book, *Hybrids of Plants and of Ghosts* (Princeton University Press, 1980).

Introduction

1. Adapted from Paula Johanson, *Early British Poetry—"Words That Burn,"* (Berkeley Heights, N.J.: Enslow Publishers, Inc.), 2010.

Chapter 1. Theodore Roethke

1. "A Roethke Chronology," *Modern American Poetry*, n.d., <http://www.english.illinois.edu/MAPS/poets/m_r/roethke/chronology.htm> (February 21, 2009).

2. James Knisely, "Theodore Roethke Remembered," *HistoryLink.org: The Online Encyclopedia of Washington State History,* June 21, 2002, <http://www.historylink.org/essays/output.cfm?file_id=3857> (February 21, 2009).

3. Theodore Roethke, *On Poetry and Craft* (Port Townsend, Wash.: Copper Canyon Press, 1965, 2001), p. 51.

Chapter 2. Elizabeth Bishop

1. Elizabeth Bishop, *The Collected Prose* (New York: Farrar, Straus and Giroux, 1984), pp. xii-xiii.

2. Brett C. Millier, *Elizabeth Bishop: A Life and the Memory of It* (Berkeley: University of California Press, 1993), p. 517.

3. Elizabeth Bishop, *One Art: Letters* (New York: Farrar, Straus and Giroux, 1994), p. 146.

4. George Plimpton, ed., *Poets at Work: The Paris Review Interviews* (New York: Viking Penguin, 1989), p. 112.

Chapter 3. William Stafford
1. William Stafford, *Writing the Australian Crawl* (Ann Arbor: University of Michigan Press, 1978), p. 10.

2. William Stafford, *Crossing Unmarked Snow* (Ann Arbor: University of Michigan Press, 1998), p. 94.

3. Stafford, p. 10.

4. Kim Stafford, *Early Morning: Remembering My Father* (Saint Paul, Minn.: Graywolf Press, 2002), p. 63.

5. Peter Stitt, *The World's Hieroglyphic Beauty: Five American Poets* (Athens: University of Georgia Press, 1985), p. 84.

Chapter 4. Robert Lowell
1. Dana Gioia, David Mason, and Meg Schoerke, *Twentieth-Century American Poetry* (New York: McGraw-Hill, 2004), p. 550.

2. Thomas Parkinson, *Robert Lowell: A Collection of Critical Essays* (Englewood Cliffs, N.J.: Prentice-Hall, Inc., 1968), p. 133.

3. Steven Gould Axelrod, *Robert Lowell: Life and Art* (Princeton, N.J.: Princeton University Press, 1978), pp. 117–118.

4. John Hollander, "Robert Lowell's New Book," from Jonathan Price, ed., *Critics on Robert Lowell: Readings in Literary Criticisms: 17* (Coral Gables, Fla.: University of Miami Press, 1972), p. 67.

5. Robert Lowell, "On 'Skunk Hour,'" from Thomas Parkinson, ed., *Robert Lowell: A Collection of Critical Essays* (Englewood Cliffs, N.J.: Prentice-Hall, Inc., 1968), p. 132.

Chapter 5. Gwendolyn Brooks

1. Harold Bloom, ed., *Gwendolyn Brooks: Bloom's BioCritiques* (Philadelphia: Chelsea House Publishers, 2005), p. 12.

2. Ibid., pp. 40–41.

3. Ibid., p. 24.

4. "On 'We Real Cool,'" *Modern American Poetry*, n.d., <http://www.english.uiuc.edu/maps/poets/a_f/brooks/werealcool.htm> (March 16, 2009).

Chapter 6. Richard Wilbur

1. 1995 Interview with Richard Wilbur, from *Image: A Journal of the Arts and Religion*, Issue #12, Winter 1995, 1998–2000, Center for Religious Humanism, Modern American Poetry, n.d., <http://www.english.uiuc.edu/maps/poets/s_z/wilbur/imageinterview.htm> (July 8, 2008).

2. Donald Hill, *Richard Wilbur* (New Haven, Conn.: Twayne Publishers, Inc., 1967), p. 121.

3. Dana Gioia, "Dana Gioia Online," 2001, <http://www.danagioia.net/essays/ewilbur.htm> (July 8, 2008).

4. Michelle Gillett, "A Mind of Grace: The Poet Richard Wilbur," *The Berkshires Week*, September 4, 2003, <http://www.berkshiresweek.com/090403/default.asp?id=article05> (July 8, 2008).

5. Theodore Roethke, *On Poetry and Craft* (Port Townsend, Wash.: Copper Canyon Press, 1965, 2001), p. 182.

6. 1995 Interview with Richard Wilbur, from *Image: A Journal of the Arts and Religion*, (July 8, 2008).

Chapter 7. Allen Ginsberg

1. Eliot Katz, "Radical Eyes: Political Poetics and 'Howl,'" Jason Shinder, ed., *The Poem That Changed America: "Howl" Fifty Years Later* (New York: Farrarr, Straus and Giroux, 2006), p. 187.

2. Marjorie Perloff, "'Howl' and the Language of Modernism," Jason Shinder, ed., *The Poem That Changed America: "Howl" Fifty Years Later* (New York: Farrar, Straus and Giroux, 2006), p. 36.

Chapter 8. W. S. Merwin

1. Billy Collins, "American Idyll; An elegiac poet who knows baseball as well as death," *Washington Post*, April 16, 2006, p. T.03.

2. Cheri Davis, *W. S. Merwin* (Boston: Twayne Publishers, 1981), p. 76.

3. Ibid., p. 21.

Chapter 9. Sylvia Plath

1. Dana Gioia, David Mason, and Meg Schoerke, *Twentieth-Century American Poetry* (New York: McGraw-Hill, 2004), p. 761.

2. Anne Stevenson, *Bitter Fame: A Life of Sylvia Plath* (Boston: Mariner Books, 1998).

3. Sylvia Plath, interviewed by Peter Orr, on October 30, 1962, *Modern American Poetry*, n.d., <http://www.english.uiuc.edu/maps/poets/m_r/plath/orrinterview.htm> and <http://sylviaplath.de/plath/orrinterview.html> (July 8, 2008).

Chapter 10. Billy Collins

1. Joel Whitney, "A Brisk Walk: Billy Collins in Conversation," *The Academy of American Poets*, n.d., <http://www.poets.org/viewmedia.php/prmMID/19796> (July 8, 2008).

2. Ibid.

3. Ibid.

Chapter 11. Louise Glück

1. Dana Gioia, David Mason, and Meg Schoerke, *Twentieth-Century American Poetry* (New York: McGraw-Hill, 2004), p. 925.

2. Articles on "Louise Glück: Image and Emotion," *The Associated Press*, <http://www.artstomp.com/gluck/news.htm> (July 8, 2008).

3. Joanne Feit Diehl, ed., *On Louise Glück: Change What You See* (Ann Arbor: University of Michigan Press, 2005), p. 183.

4. Articles on "Louise Glück: Image and Emotion."

5. Tony Hoagland, "Three Tenors: Glück, Hass, Pinsky, and the Deployment of Talent," *American Poetry Review*, 03603709, July/August 2003, vol. 32, issue 4, <http://findarticles.com/p/articles/mi_qa3692/is_200307/ai_n9244249/?tag=content;col1> (June 5, 2009).

6. Louise Glück, *Proofs & Theories: Essays on Poetry* (New York: Ecco, 1994), p. 74.

GLOSSARY

alliteration—The repetition of the same or similar sounds at the beginning of words.

assonance—The repetition of vowel sounds.

confessional poetry— Poetry that reveals personal, sometimes painful or unflattering information.

consonance—Harmony or agreement of sounds in words.

couplet—A pair of lines, often of the same length, that rhyme and form a complete thought.

end-rhyme—A pattern in which the last words of lines rhyme.

end-stopped—A poetic line that ends at the same place as a sentence within the poem.

enjambment—The continuation of a sentence from one line of a poem to the next without a pause.

iambic—A poetic rhythm consisting of an unstressed syllable followed by a stressed syllable.

imagery—Figurative language.

metaphor—A figure of speech in which a word is compared to another to suggest similarity between them.

meter—The measure of systematically arranged rhythm in poetry, in units of syllables within a line, with one stressed syllable and three, two, one, or no unstressed syllables.

persona—The narrator of a poem, created by the author.

poet laureate—A recognized eminent poet appointed to promote poetry and to represent a country or locality.

rhyme scheme—A pattern of rhyming words, often placed at the end of the poetic line.

simile—A figure of speech in which two things are compared using the terms "like" or "as."

slant rhyme—A rhyme scheme in which the vowels or consonants of stressed syllables are identical, as in cane/blame and years/yours. Also called half-rhyme.

stanza—A verse or set of lines grouped together and set apart from the rest of the poem, like a paragraph in prose writing.

surrealism—A style of art and literature (developed mainly in the twentieth century) that expresses the images of unconscious or subconscious thoughts and dreams.

Further Reading

Lathbury, Roger. *American Modernism (1910–1945)*. New York: Facts on File, 2006.

McClatchy, J. D., ed. *The Vintage Book of Contemporary American Poetry*. New York: Vintage, 2003.

Parisi, Joseph, and Stephen Young, eds. *The Poetry Anthology*. Chicago: Ivan R. Dee, 2004.

Rosenberg, Liz, editor. *The Invisible Ladder: An Anthology of Contemporary American Poems for Young Readers*. New York: Henry Holt & Co., 2006.

Internet Addresses

The Academy of American Poets

<http://www.poets.org>

Modern American Poetry, an Online Journal and Multimedia Companion to Anthology of Modern American Poetry

<http://www.english.uiuc.edu/maps/>

Poetry Foundation

<http://www.poetryfoundation.org/>

INDEX

Permissions

"My Papa's Waltz", copyright 1942 by Hearst Magazines, Inc., "Old Florist", copyright 1946 by Harper & Brothers, "The Waking", copyright 1945 by Theodore Roethke, "Epidermal Macabre", copyright 1932 by Theodore Roethke, from COLLECTED POEMS OF THEODORE ROETHKE by Theodore Roethke. Used by permission of Doubleday, a division of Random House, Inc.

"Sandpiper", "The Shampoo", and "One Art" from THE COMPLETE POEMS, 1927–1979 by Elizabeth Bishop. Copyright © 1979, 1983 by Alice Helen Methfessel. Reprinted by permission of Farrar, Straus and Giroux, LLC.

William Stafford, "Fifteen," "The Little Girl by the Fence at School," "School Play," and "Your Life" from The Way It Is: New and Selected Poems. Copyright © 1966, 1987, 1991, 1998 by William Stafford and the Estate of William Stafford. Reprinted with the permission of Graywolf Press, Minneapolis, Minnesota, www.graywolfpress.org.

"Skunk Hour", "For Sale", and "Grandparents" from COLLECTED POEMS OF ROBERT LOWELL by Robert Lowell. Copyright © 1959 by Robert Lowell, copyright renewed 2003 by Harriet Lowell and Sheridan Lowell. Reprinted by permission of Farrar, Straus and Giroux, LLC.

"Kitchenette Building," copyright © 1945 by Gwendolyn Brooks Blakely, copyright renewed © 2003 by Nora Brooks Blakely; "We Real Cool," and "The Crazy Woman," copyright © 1960 by Gwendolyn Brooks Blakely, copyright renewed © 2003 by Nora Brooks Blakely; "Big Bessie Throws Her Son Into the Street," copyright 1963 by Gwendolyn Brooks Blakely, copyright renewed © 2003 by Nora Brooks Blakely; from SELECTED POEMS OF GWENDOLYN BROOKS. Reprinted with permission.

"Love Calls Us to the Things of This World" and "Mind" from THINGS OF THIS WORLD, copyright © 1956 and renewed 1984 by Richard Wilbur; "The Pardon" from CEREMONY AND OTHER POEMS, copyright 1950 and renewed 1978 by Richard Wilbur; "Poem 23" from OPPOSITES: POEMS AND DRAWINGS, copyright © 1973 by Richard Wilbur. Reprinted by permission of Houghton Mifflin Harcourt Publishing Company.

Excerpt from "Howl" and "In back of the real" from HOWL AND OTHER POEMS by Allen Ginsberg, copyright © 1957 by Allen Ginsberg, copyright renewed © 2001 by City Lights Books; "Uptown" from PLANET NEWS by Allen Ginsberg, copyright 1968 by Allen Ginsberg, copyright renewed 2001 by City Lights Books. Reprinted by permission of HarperCollins Publishers.

"The Flight" by W. S. Merwin, copyright © 1977 by W. S. Merwin; "For the Anniversary of My Death" by W. S. Merwin, copyright © 1973 by W. S. Merwin; "Late Wonders" by W. S. Merwin, copyright © 1997 by W. S. Merwin; reprinted with permission of The Wylie Agency LLC.

"Morning Song," "The Couriers," and "Mirror" from COLLECTED POEMS by Sylvia Plath, copyright © 1963, 1981 by The Estate of Sylvia Plath. Reprinted by permission of HarperCollins Publishers.

"Boy Shooting at a Statue," "Special Glasses," and "The Student" from THE TROUBLE WITH POETRY: AND OTHER POEMS by Billy Collins, copyright © 2005 by Billy Collins; reprinted with permission of Random House, Inc.

"The Triumph of Achilles" and "Pomegranate" from THE FIRST FOUR BOOKS OF POEMS by Louise Glück, copyright © 1995 by Louise Glück; "Brown Circle" from ARARAT by Louise Glück, copyright © 1990 by Louise Glück; "Witchgrass" from THE WILD IRIS by Louise Glück, copyright © 1992 by Louise Glück; reprinted by permission of HarperCollins Publishers.